Education and Training
Chaos or Coherence?

Edited by Rob Halsall and Mike Cockett

David Fulton Publishers
London

David Fulton Publishers Ltd
2 Barbon Close, London WC1N 3JX

First published in Great Britain by
David Fulton Publishers 1996

Note: The right of Rob Halsall and Mike Cockett to be identified as the
editors of this work has been asserted by them in accordance with the
Copyright, Designs and Patents Act 1988.

Copyright © David Fulton Publishers Ltd

British Library Cataloguing in Publication Data

A catalogue record for this book is available from the British Library

ISBN 1–85346-419-8

Typeset by The Harrington Consultancy Ltd.
Printed in Great Britain by the Cromwell Press Ltd., Melksham.

Contents

Preface   v

Contributors   vi

1   Setting the Scene   1
    Rob Halsall

2   Continuity and Change in Post-Compulsory Education and
    Training Reform   11
    Denis Gleeson

3   National Vocational Qualifications – A Way Forward?   17
    Phil Hodkinson

4   Vocationalism and Vocational Courses 14–16   33
    Mike Cockett

5   Caught in the Middle – Transition at 16+   50
    Mike Cockett and John Callaghan

6   Core Skills – The Continuing Debate   73
    Rob Halsall

7   Records of Achievement – Rhetoric or Reality?   89
    Rob Halsall

8   Rationales for Student-Centred Learning   108
    David Hustler and Phil Hodkinson

9   Higher Education – A Clear Sense of Vision?   120
    Rob Halsall and David Hustler

10 Chaos or Coherence, Progression and Continuity   137
    Mike Cockett

References   143

Index   151

The Manchester Metropolitan University Education Series

Planned jointly by the University and David Fulton Publishers, this Series seeks to apply professionally-focused research to classroom learning and teaching and to other aspects of education practice. Most of the authors are based at or connected with MMU's Didsbury and Crewe and Alsager Schools of Education.

Other Series Titles

Arts Education for a Multicultural Society
John Robinson and David Hustler (with school case studies by Russell Jones and Jill Evans)
1–85346–382–5

Exploring Writing and Play in the Early Years
Nigel Hall and Anne Robinson
1–85346–379–5

Learning Contracts and Initial Teacher Education
Edited by David Hustler, Jan Peckett and Margaret Whiteley
1–85346–381–7

Writing for Publication in Education – a beginner's guide to books, journals and presentations
Nigel Hall
1–85346–380–9

Preface

Since returning to power in 1979, Tory governments have introduced sweeping changes in most aspects of educational provision in order to make institutions more accountable, to obtain better 'value for money' and to 'improve standards'. As is to be expected, the level of success of each new initiative has been variable and in many cases impossible to gauge as yet. What seems evident to us, however, is that attempts to improve and make more coherent the provision of education and training for the 14–19 age group represent one of the least successful ventures.

This book examines some of the major issues in the education and training of young people. It contributes to the debate about provision at a time when critical decisions are being made which will affect the shape of the system for many years to come. Relying on experience in organising and evaluating initiatives designed to improve the management and assessment of learning, we and our contributors aim to provide a critical commentary on current piecemeal developments. We also spell out lessons which we feel must be learnt if future developments are to lead to a genuine raising of standards. Examples are taken from work in schools, further education and higher education. They focus on the confusions, dilemmas and incoherence which face tutors and students as attempts are made to translate rhetoric into practice.

Rob Halsall and Mike Cockett
Manchester, December 1995

List of Contributors

John Callaghan was until recently Senior Tutor at St John Rigby Sixth Form College, Wigan. His responsibilities included the introduction of CPVE courses, liaison with local high schools, recruitment and induction procedures and the guidance and counselling of students as they prepared for transition to higher education or employment.

Mike Cockett is currently Research Fellow at The Manchester Metropolitan University's Didsbury School of Education. Previously he was an inspector and TVEI coordinator for Manchester LEA, following a period as coordinator of the Alternative Curriculum Strategies Project, again in Manchester.

Denis Gleeson is Professor of Education and Director of the Centre for Social Research in Education at the University of Keele. He has been involved in a number of major research projects looking at youth, school, further education and employment issues. Currently, he is researching the impact of market and employer-led forces on post-compulsory education, training and policy.

Rob Halsall is Research Development Manager at the Didsbury School of Education. His particular interests are management of change, 14–19 education generally and developments in higher education. Together with David Hustler, he has been involved in evaluation of TVEI, recording achievement and guidance and learner autonomy in higher education.

Phil Hodkinson is Principal Lecturer at MMU's Crewe School of Education. He has conducted several research studies of post-compulsory education and training, including a major investigation of one of the pilot Training Credits schemes. He has written widely on post-16 issues.

David Hustler is Professor of Education at the Didsbury School of Education. He has led a number of evaluation teams looking at TVEI, flexible learning, recording achievement in higher education and guidance and learner autonomy in higher education. His particular interests are teaching and learning styles and learning environments. He has edited and contributed to a variety of books concerned with secondary and post-compulsory education.

1

Setting The Scene

Rob Halsall

INTRODUCTION

It is not difficult to make the argument that 14+ provision, especially post-16 education and training and the continuity of learners' experiences, was far from coherent throughout the 1970s and early 1980s. It can also be seen as having failed to either motivate or meet the aspirations of large numbers of students and as having failed to ensure an adequate supply of sufficiently educated and trained people for society at large, including business and industry.

Post-16, there was a mass of largely occupation-specific vocational and technical qualifications, with little in the way of clear progression paths either within or across these. As Wolf (1995) has pointed out there was, until the introduction of National Vocational Qualifications (NVQs), no formal overall structure for 'non-academic' education and training. The statutory bodies concerned with industrial training were highly autonomous and numerous, many guarding their independence jealously. What there was in common was a lack of understanding by many students, employers and universities of what different awards meant and how they related to each other. At 14–16, Local Education Authorities (LEAs) and schools had responded in a wide variety of ways to provide a curriculum for their youngsters and there was a dual qualification system of O-levels and CSEs which served to narrow progression opportunities for many students.

It is also clear that British educational and training achievements were lagging behind those of most other industrialised nations. For example, in 1987 only 35% of 16–18 year olds were in full-time education and training as compared with 51% in Australia, 77% in Japan and The Netherlands and 82% in Belgium (DES, 1991).

TORY EDUCATION AND TRAINING POLICY

Tory governments have attempted to remedy this 'mess', largely motivated by their view, apparent in recent White Papers (1994, 1995) that a coherent and reformed education and training system is vital in 'helping business to win' the economic battle with overseas competitors. This is nothing new, but rarely has the link between education and training and the economy been so powerfully articulated and pursued. Great play is made, in the 1994 White Paper, of the perception that the UK has been good at educating our most able students and that the 'best' of our schools, colleges and universities are 'world class', but that raising the average level of aspiration and attainment in education and training is necessary. I shall briefly review some key steps that have been taken post-1979 in order to achieve this aim.

First, a three-track qualification system has been established. Because the UK has secured, it seems, excellent results from those choosing the most academic options, the GCSE/AS/A-level track is to be retained. However, to raise the motivation, aspirations and attainments of others, alternative tracks of work-based NVQs and school/college-based General NVQs have been introduced. These were originally confined to the post-16 sector but now GNVQs are to be available at Key Stage 4. A division of agencies was established in relation to these qualification routes, academic programmes being 'located' with the Department for Education and the School Curriculum and Assessment Authority, and vocational programmes 'located' with the Employment Department and the National Council for Vocational Qualifications (NCVQ). Although the Employment Department has disappeared, with its training brief being absorbed by a new, unified Department for Education and Employment, and although there is every likelihood that the assessment agencies will merge, there is still no suggestion of a unified qualification system. Dearing's interim review of education and training (Dearing, 1995) proposes a common family of national certificates and a unified *framework* of qualifications but there is no suggestion that the different qualification tracks should be radically reformed. In the words of the Liberal Democrats' education spokesman, Don Foster, the proposals are 'half a loaf … half-way down the road of integrating vocational and academic qualifications' (TES, 1995).

Second, 'standards' and targets have been set in a variety of forms. At one level, National Targets for Training and Education (NETTs) have been established. These embrace intentions concerning the percentage of people, both in full-time education and training and in (or out of) work, to gain academic or vocational qualifications at different levels, as well as ambitions concerning the development in individuals of self-reliance, flexibility and breadth. A National Advisory Council has been formed to monitor progress toward the targets. At other levels, the curriculum framework of vocational courses is provided by statements of competence and a new General Diploma has been proposed for those who gain GCSEs at grade C or above in mathematics, science and English, together with any other two GCSEs at C+ or their vocational equivalent.

Third, education and training have been increasingly privatised or semi-privatised and the notion of competitiveness has been seen as equally applicable to this area as to business. Thus, a variety of Acts has led to the introduction of the local management of schools, budgetary devolvement, open enrolment, the incorporation of post-16 and higher education institutions, the inspection of schools by private inspection teams, league tables, failing schools legislation, grant-maintained schools with their separate Funding Agency, City Technology Colleges and a privatised careers service. Among the outcomes of the above is competition for students between different schools, between colleges and schools, between Training and Enterprise Councils and colleges and between colleges and universities. There is even competition between LEAs and their 'own' schools.

Fourth, several work-related developments have been introduced. The Technical and Vocational Education Initiative (TVEI) aims to equip 14–18 year olds with 'broad based characteristics such as enterprise and initiative and...valuable work experience'. Formal links between schools and business have been promoted through Education Business Partnerships, Compacts and a Teacher Placement Service and Youth Training has been established as a route for youngsters leaving school at 16 or 17. The government is also introducing Modern Apprenticeships which will offer work-based training to at least NVQ level 3. Most recently, the government has proposed more work-based education for 'demotivated' 14–16 year olds, possibly occupying up to half of their studies.

Finally, the importance of broad and balanced programmes of study has been stressed. Here, the introduction of a National Curriculum has been seen as central to the education of 5–16 year olds, both in its original form and in the 'slimmed down' post-Dearing version. As regards the post-16 sector, where students undertake a narrower curriculum diet within both academic and vocational courses, the importance of addressing a range of 'generic' skills has been emphasised. Thus, we can point to the core skills units and grading themes of GNVQs; proposals in the 1995 White Paper for the testing of all A-level candidates in the skills of literacy, numeracy and information technology and for the development of schemes to improve students' negotiating and decision-making skills; and the encouragement given to post-16 institutions to adopt the National Record of Achievement which is statutory for all 16-year-old school leavers.

It is, perhaps, with this last set of developments that some would see the link between education and training strategies and the economy most clearly, especially in the context of a post-Fordist analysis of economic organisation. Whereas Fordist production is concerned with standardised products for a mass market of consumers, post-Fordism is about the rapid production, delivery and consumption of goods and services which are aimed at relatively small, niche markets. Here, the focus is on providing the products that consumers want to buy rather than on making them want to purchase what is on offer. There are implications for the necessary flexibility and adaptability of both plant and the workforce.

In relation to the latter, Murray (1989) suggests that post-Fordism in manufacturing is most clearly demonstrated in Japanese car companies where the workforce has been transformed from that which operated in a Fordist system. Whereas in the latter the worker is basically an unskilled or semi-skilled machine operator with little responsibility for what he or she does, in the post-Fordist context workers are viewed as multi-skilled and their tasks include not only manufacture but the improvement of the products and the production processes. They are given responsibility and, as members of work groups, are delegated day-to-day autonomy. 'Teams linking departments horizontally have replaced the rigid verticality of Fordist bureaucracies' (Murray, 1989 p:46). Here lies the emphasis on 'generic' skills: all workers need to be effective team members, good communicators, self-reliant, problem solvers and, at least to some degree, autonomous.

ABOUT THIS BOOK

This book offers the perspectives of its contributors on the elements of current education and training policy as outlined above. It does so under the broad heading of *Chaos or Coherence*. The government believes that it has adopted a more coherent approach to education and training than has previously been the case. However, we believe that the strategies pursued raise a number of issues, tensions and contradictions which can be seen as seriously undermining the governments' attempts to achieve coherence. These, of course, are an inevitable part of managing change and those caught up in the process of change are invariably ambivalent about it. As Macfarlane points out, 'Even the strongest advocates of reform may succumb to expediency and an occasional reluctance to abandon tried and trusted methods' (1993:xv). While we argue, in this book, that recent government efforts have failed to achieve the coherent system sought, we acknowledge the difficulties involved. Indeed, we doubt whether it is possible to achieve such an aim. The consequence of working and living in complex circumstances, and of never having sufficient information to predict individual, group or societal futures, is that we must live with chaos. However, there is a distinction between deterministic and culpable chaos. The former is marked by attempts to address structural anomalies in as coherent a way as possible. This demands a flexible and responsive approach and it demands dialogue. It is here that more searching questions can be raised regarding government policy.

The matter of dialogue has been important to the genesis of the book. First, dialogue between the various contributors who have a shared commitment generally to an education and training system which is, first and foremost, for the benefit of our students, their learning and their progression in the system. They also have a shared commitment to a number of the more specific initiatives within education and training that are visited in the book. Here, we would stress that although a critical stance is adopted in relation to these, that is because we are passionate advocates who believe that critical debate is essential if the promises these initiatives hold out are to be realised.

Second, dialogue between the contributors and a wider audience has been important. We recognised that debate amongst ourselves was insufficient. Although we could identify issues and raise questions, we were not sure if these would strike a chord elsewhere. The decision was taken, therefore, to invite practitioners and others involved in 14–19 education and training to a set of seminars and discussions led by us in order to share perceptions. Because, for us, matters of progression and continuity were key issues there was a particular concern to have cross-sectoral representation. Over 40 people attended the seminars. They included school TVEI co-ordinators, LEA or college co-ordinators of Records of Achievement or Core Skills, headteachers and college senior management team members and higher education colleagues. The result was that a chord *was* struck. Even though many of the participants were 'charged' to implement new systems or this or that initiative and were, naturally, preoccupied with the day-to-day demands of doing so, few were oblivious to the issues, tensions and contradictions that were raised by us. Not all shared our perceptions, certainly not on all of the topics debated. Another result of the day was that *we* learned much and we feel that this learning has influenced the final product, this book.

Clearly, we hope that our contributions, informed as they are, at least in part, by the seminar participants, will represent a useful element in further dialogue on the issues and questions they raise. Our primary 'audience' is all of those people involved in 14–19 education and training, especially those in a middle or senior management or professional development role. It is our hope that this book will go some way in enabling them to step back a little from their day-to-day responsibilities in order to develop their own constructive critiques. This, in turn, might have some cumulative effect in alerting policy makers to some of the concerns about, and suggestions for, 14–19 education and training that those involved in it have to offer. Of course, we also hope that our own critique will address policy makers directly.

AN OVERVIEW OF THE CHAPTERS

Gleeson acknowledges that further education and training have now become an integral part of mass education and welcomes the fact that they are opening up the range of opportunities for people first envisaged in the Crowther Report. He also welcomes the fact that the government has established guidelines necessary to achieve reform of vocational and education training. However, Gleeson queries the likely success of a policy which is driven by market principles, involves the transference of the curriculum knowledge base from professionals to quangos and various agencies, embraces competing initiatives and competing institutions and favours parity of esteem between different qualifications, rather than a unified system of post-16 provision. Effective change, he argues, needs to be based on giving greater voice to all partners including youth, teachers and community concerns and engaging with the culture of schools and colleges, on a learner-oriented rather than received pedagogy, on seeing students as learners rather than as customers and on a belief in the equal importance of all young peoples' education.

Hodkinson focuses on NVQs which he views not only as a major element in the expansion of opportunities referred to by Gleeson, but also as an initiative which has helped transform thinking about vocational and education training. However, several problems are identified which stem from an over-simplified approach. In particular, he suggests that there are a number of fallacies underpinning the NCVQ competence framework and argues that, owing to the drive to achieve NETTS, inadequate consideration has been given to the quality of the learning process. Both issues relate to Gleeson's concern for learner-oriented rather than received pedagogy. Hodkinson does not argue for the abolition of NVQs but, rather, for attention to their shortcomings and he offers suggestions as to how these might be addressed.

Cockett, in addressing vocationalism – a belief in the value of vocational provision – at Key Stage 4 recognises that some authors have argued against the development of vocational options in schools on ideological grounds. More pragmatically, he suggests that there are mechanisms in, and characteristics of, schools and their communities which serve to operate against their success. Cockett argues that it is because such issues have not been sufficiently addressed in past attempts to introduce vocational courses and course elements that they have been largely unsuccessful. Throughout the chapter there is a particular concern for how the education system is failing the lower and lowest attaining students on whom the vocational options are principally targeted. The central point made is that the provision of 'alternative' curricula does not change the wider context which defines low attainers as such and thereby ensures that they continue to under-achieve.

Those students who have not been amongst the highest achievers are a continuing concern in the contribution by Cockett and Callaghan, especially those who represent the large 'middle band' which just fails to reach A-level entry standard at the age of 16. This chapter differs from the others in the book in that it is based on an empirical study carried out by the authors which focuses on the attitudes of a small sample of this middle group of students at a time when they had progressed to post-16 provision, mainly intermediate/level 2 vocational programmes. Doubt is cast on the efficacy of the National Curriculum in motivating youngsters and providing them with a sense of achievement, in serving as an adequate basis for progression and, indeed, in actually providing a broad and balanced curriculum. A key factor here is the GCSE grading system and how it is perceived.

The next two chapters by Halsall have as their main focus the question of whether the core skills and recording achievement initiatives are achieving, or can achieve, their primary purposes. Core skills can be seen as adding breadth to the curriculum, as a response to post-Fordist economic organisation and as a means of bridging the academic–vocational divide, not least by addressing the issue of progression by way of the notion of transferability. Doubts are expressed concerning the rationale for the skills which have been identified as 'core', whether they can be seen as transferable, whether the core skills initiative can be anything other than mere tinkering with a disunified education and training system and whether the location of these skills in what is a largely behaviourist model of competences is helpful. However, in the absence of a unified qualification system, it is acknowledged that the initiative, if modified, does have the potential for reducing the divisive treatment of students, not least in relation to helping them to maximise their learning potential.

Given the skills involved in the processes underlying the production of Records of Achievement (ROAs), there is considerable overlap between this initiative and a number of the core skills. Halsall explores the potential benefits of ROAs: an 'antidote' to external examinations, the provision of more comprehensive and appropriate information to end-users, the raising of motivation and self-esteem and the furtherance of student-centred and autonomous learning. The evidence for such outcomes is then reviewed. This suggests a rather mixed and patchy picture which falls some way short of reflecting the wealth of favourable opinions offered by enthusiasts. Moreover, a number of tensions surrounding ROAs are discussed, to do with privacy, ownership and control. It is argued that unless these are addressed, and until certain other conditions are met, including that relating to progression, the potential benefits of ROAs will not be realised on a greater scale than has been the case to date.

The chapter by Hustler and Hodkinson follows up on student-centred learning and learner autonomy. They suggest that there seems to be a widespread belief, across a number of communities involved in 14+ education and training, in the appropriateness of the development of these, but then point to the existence of differing bases for this commitment. Here, different sets of arguments for student-centred learning and learner autonomy are explored, to do with democratisation, effective learning and preparation for the world of work. Hustler and Hodkinson suggest that, although these arguments interrelate, there are differences between them and they argue that it is incumbent on advocates of student-centred learning to be explicit concerning the reasons underlying their commitment and, indeed, to allow students access to these. As in the previous chapter, the authors also raise questions concerning what evidence there is to support propositions about the outcomes of student-centred learning, though they recognise that there are certain arguments which do not stand or fall in relation to evidence.

The penultimate chapter asks if, as advanced throughout the book, there is confusion and uncertainty surrounding 14–19 education and training, what of higher education (HE)? It can be argued that for many years this sector has played a significant role in helping to create, or at least sustain, a disunified and hierarchical system in the pre-HE sectors. It has, for example, been a key influence on the retention of A-levels, on the GCSE grading system and on students' choices of qualification routes and of options within those. As Halsall and Hustler indicate, though, HE itself is now subject to several forces for change, some of which are those evident in schools and colleges. These are impacting on the curriculum and on teaching and learning to a greater or lesser extent both within and between institutions, leading to similar confusions and uncertainties as in the 14–19 sector. However, the authors suggest the likelihood of a clearer mix of different types of university emerging where differences between them will be more significant than differences within a particular institution. This is likely to produce greater coherence within the sector, but might this represent a parallel with the post-1944 structure of secondary modern, technical and grammar schools, which in turn could reinforce the divisiveness and confusion that we argue is to be found in 14–19 education and training?

Finally, in concluding the book, Cockett explores further the notion that, whilst it might be impossible to arrive at a coherent system, there is a distinction between deterministic and culpable chaos. He argues that some elements of coherence are essential to address the structural anomalies which we know about. For Cockett, and indeed for the contributors at large, the key element of coherence is that relating to progression. In a fragmented and constantly changing system, continuity of experience might not be achievable, but progression must be. The challenge is to ensure that, whatever form or forms the system takes, each phase of learning builds on the previous phase and that students are presented with new and 'deepening' possibilities. What must be avoided, Cockett urges, is 'a system of cul-de-sacs involving constant retreat before redirection'.

2

Continuity and Change in Post-Compulsory Education and Training Reform

Denis Gleeson

AT THE CENTRE OF POLICY DEBATE

In the past decade post-compulsory education and training has attracted the interest of government, trade unions, employer representatives, educationists and the increased participation of students themselves. Much recent attention has followed on the influential government White Papers (e.g. 1994), which acknowledge that decades of failure to invest in post-compulsory education and training, in both good and bad times, have left Britain with a vicious circle of low skills, low wages and low productivity, and also with one of the least educated and trained workforces in the industrial world. Indeed, a new-found consensus has emerged among previously antagonistic partners – trade unionists, Confederation of British Industry, Labour Party, Examination Bodies and Government – that nothing short of a *skills revolution* is needed to break this vicious circle and arrest Britain's downward economic spiral.

In various and often contradictory ways, such apparent new realism has placed post-compulsory education and training at the centre of policy debate. From being a relative backwater of mainstream education, further education (FE) and training, traditionally viewed as the Cinderella or handmaiden of British industry, has increasingly become an integral part of mass education itself. In recent years, improvements in GCSE and A-level results, the take-up of General National Vocational Qualifications (GNVQs) and increased participation rates, bode well for the passage of post-16 education and training reform. Despite the lack of enthusiasm for science, there are encouraging signs that more young people are taking advantage of the broadening post-16 curriculum framework, with its promise of parity of esteem between academic and vocational qualifications, improved higher education (HE) access and job opportunities. Moreover, with GNVQ now on stream and heralded in some quarters as *the alternative route*, there are historic signs that further education and training is, at last, opening up the range of opportunities first envisaged by Crowther (1959).

If, in official terms, the rationale for post-16 reform is to do with re-skilling the economy for the twenty-first century, the question arises, how will market forces and qualifications-led reform achieve this? According to Maclure (1991) the dire economic crises of the late 1980s and early 1990s have led to an emerging policy assumption that all young people should continue in education and training to at least 19, and be linked with the planned expansion of FE and HE. As a foundation, four basic policy assumptions are deemed necessary to drive the new reforms. They are two routes for 16–19s (academic and vocational); two modes of provision (full and part-time); over-lapping qualifications (A-levels and GNVQs); and two sets of destinations (HE and work). However, to be successful these policy assumptions must, according to the government, be linked to nationally agreed training priorities, targets and standards, encompassing:

- centralised reform of national vocational qualifications in more systematic and competence-led fashion, linked with national and international training targets;
- supporting progression between school, college, work and HE;
- giving more attention to post-16 provision, self-governance, participation and retention;
- sustaining local, regional and national industrial and commercial partnerships;
- legislation designed to create and sustain an education and training market, for example the Education Reform Act, 1988 (ERA), the FE and HE Act, 1992 and the Education Act, 1994.

SKILLS FOR THE TWENTY-FIRST CENTURY

Given the post-16 policy vacuum pervading since Crowther (1959), such acknowledgement of the guidelines necessary to achieve national vocational and education training reform represents a significant step forward. On this basis one might reasonably expect to discern a clear policy direction following on the 1994 White Paper. It is, however, at this point that any sense of a policy *rapprochement* between the different parties disappears. Thus, while a growing consensus may exist about what the problem is (i.e. the vicious circle), there is no agreement about the solution or resolution of the policy issues involved. In reality the policy is one of no policy: instead, a vision of the future is enshrined in legislation designed to deregulate, devolve and diversify existing post-16 provision.

Following on ERA (1988), the FE and HE Act (1992) and the Education Act (1994), future policy direction in the 1990s is now driven by market principles and deregulation. Effectively, the three Acts have combined to break a municipal or public service view of school and further education, linking schools and colleges with LEAs within the spirit of the 1944 Education Act. Institutional autonomy and corporate status now place institutions in the market place apparently freed of external constraint. Self-governance, Training and Enterprise Councils (TECs), Training Credits, Enterprise, Business Partnerships and new rules of governance and funding now have a major impact on school and post-16 provision, rendering education and training more market-led, client-centred, entrepreneurial and responsive to industrial and commercial needs.

This is envisaged to be achieved in two interrelated ways: first, by post-16 institutions becoming less course-led and more student-centred; and, second, by colleges anticipating new markets and funding arrangements with the Further Education Funding Council (FEFC), TECs, business, industrial, commercial and related lead bodies. In this way, recent legislation seeks to not only centrally promote an expanded post-16 education and training system, driven more by private than public enterprise, but also to ensure delivery of National Training Targets, associated with improved skill levels, GNVQs and increased student participation and better value for money. In other words, the new arrangements of further education and training will redistribute the subsidy from the supplier (the colleges), to the customer (most likely industry or commerce) and the consumer (the student). In so doing, reducing unit costs, competition and responding to market needs are seen to encourage the efficiency, responsiveness and flexibility of institutions.

If, on the surface, such an approach appears radical and student-centred, it has much in common with other deregulated aspects of Government industrial relations' legislation. In recent years much of this has been concerned with curbing the influence of trade unions, local authorities and health and safety bodies, and with abolishing Wages' Councils, Industrial Training Boards and training levies. If this ostensibly is concerned with freeing up the market, it also represents a political mechanism for centralising state control. In education and training terms this involves transferring the knowledge base of the curriculum from professionals to other bodies (employers, TECs, governors, lead bodies, training agencies, the National Council for Vocational Qualifications, FEFC and so forth). Moreover, reducing the role of LEAs, teachers and unions to residual functions, creating managerial systems charged with accountability and establishing institutions as financially autonomous (with formula-driven limits), effectively ensures the responsiveness of schools and colleges to external agencies and agendas. The question is, has the new vocationalism worked? Much, of course, depends on what one means by *works*.

In addressing this, a question remains about the commitment of employers to employer and market-led education and training reform. In the UK the likelihood of employer funds flowing into the system looks increasingly slim, given the small chance to win at local level a battle over training levies and student grants that has not been fought nationally.

The question remains, too, can the inevitability of change be left to voluntarism and markets alone? In terms of the UK experience the answer to this question is a big 'if'. According to the CBI (1989) '...only if young people, educationists, government, unions and employers come together to make it happen'. In response to both questions, the problem is how can the parties come together, given the proliferation of quangos and initiatives competing in the market place? Here, the local management of schools, corporate status and Funding Council activity (linking 'bums on seats', examination passes and student retention) bring forward the necessity of making uncomfortable decisions for schools and colleges about how to allocate resources and how to compete, rather than co-operate, with other establishments.

In such a climate of doubt and uncertainty about the future it is perhaps not surprising that much energy is expended in institutional competition: in vying for students who come with a price on their head, as opposed to developing quality schools and colleges designed to serve the best interests of their students. This, coupled with the return to an examination-based GCSE, continued conflict over National Curricular assessment, deregulation of LEA control and

Government hegemony of initial teacher education and the continuing professional development of teachers, has placed retrenchment over change on the agenda. This, alongside the failure to reform A-levels adequately and provide a unified system of post-16 provision, ensures that parity of esteem, rather than equality, remains firmly on the Conservative government's agenda.

TOWARD A NEW EDUCATIONAL SETTLEMENT?

Real and lasting educational reform cannot be subordinated to the causal determinants of economy, or traditions of hierarchy and social exclusion. Genuine alternatives must embrace an active view of citizenship which links partnership and empowerment in personal education and economic relations, beyond market, qualification and employer-led considerations. This demands recognition that the driving force of reform is the quality of *teaching and learning* in school and post-compulsory education. It also involves realisation that education, learning, society and work are synonymous, not separate, entities. Principles of democracy and social justice are involved here, in terms of how education and training helps shape, rather than passively reflect on, the future of industrial society. Here, a central task will be to establish a unified national qualification system, challenging traditional notions of equivalence and parity of esteem.

The crucial importance of the quality of teaching and learning as the precursor to (rather than the appendage of) outcomes, targets, competences and performance indicators needs to be recognised. This, linked with employment and career-related, rather than employer and business-led, reform is a pressing issue. It involves challenging what Evans (1992) has described as the 'private governance of public money' as a basis of education policy: embracing broader views of the student as learner rather than as customer, or skills carrier. It also involves principles of inclusion rather than exclusion of key partners in education and training, giving greater voice to youth, teachers, unions, parents, local authority and community concerns. In short, Conservative new realism needs replacing with a *new coherence*, one based on investment in education rather than reliance on initiative and market-led considerations.

The deeper message here is that there is a need to go beyond both

1944 and Thatcherite settlements, the challenge being to generate a new 'Third Education settlement' which combines conceptions of social unity and community, with competitiveness and productivity. According to Donald (1992), it is essential to establish any such new settlement on principles of '…participation and distributive justice rather than simple egalitarianism and on cultural heterogeneity rather than a shared humanity'. Here, a key feature will be in the transition from a received to a learner-oriented pedagogy which radically redefines the *social relationship* between learning, earning and economic growth. If anything has been learned from 15 years of Conservative education reform it is that future education and training policy which fails to engage with young people, the culture of the school, college and teaching profession, is unlikely to achieve meaningful reform. Not until education policy and practice is driven by a belief that the *equal importance of all young people's education is equally in all our interests* will more of them believe that they can equally benefit from the goods that schools and colleges have to offer.

3

National Vocational Qualifications – A Way Forward?

Phil Hodkinson

INTRODUCTION

National Vocational Qualifications (NVQs) were designed to meet a very real need. In the early 1980s, Vocational Education and Training (VET) in Britain was in a mess. Training was not taken seriously by many British firms and there was a jungle of vocational qualifications, many of which were narrowly occupationally specific. The apprentice system was rapidly declining and, even at its height, had only served the needs of a minority of industries, mainly male-dominated craft trades. British educational and training achievements were well behind those of most of our competitor nations. Furthermore, it was already apparent that the number of unskilled and semi-skilled jobs was declining, so that skilled labour was forming an ever-increasing proportion of the British labour market.

In this context, something dramatic had to be done, and NVQs were certainly that. The NVQ revolution has brought qualifications within the reach of many workers who had no chance of achieving them before. It has also been largely responsible for transformations of thinking about VET that have spread, with clear benefit, right through much of further and higher education. Two such transformations stand out. The first is the acceptance of work-based learning and assessment. The second is the use of the Accreditation of Prior Experience and Learning. The latter is now widely used by higher education teams who are often unaware that the original idea and much of the early development work took place within the National Council for Vocational Qualifications (NCVQ).

That NVQs have achieved so much is greatly to the credit of a relatively small group of committed enthusiasts, perhaps the most prominent of whom were Gilbert Jessup and Graham Debling. This group have changed the face of VET in Britain, a major achievement based on a dedicated single mindedness and fixity of purpose. In what follows, many aspects of the NVQ vision and emerging structure are subjected to a critique but the criticisms should be read in the context of the undoubted achievements of NVQs, for they are both sides of the same coin. The criticism is meant to be constructive. Some of the problems of the current NVQ system are identified to suggest some key issues which should be addressed, and to give a few pointers to possible ways forward. In doing this, NVQs are considered in three different ways. First, some of the basic principles upon which they were designed and developed are challenged. Second, evidence is examined from a recent research study about the relationships between NVQs and training quality, in the current British VET context. Then, some lessons are drawn from work done with competence-based approaches, in teacher education, youth and community work and social work, which were not designed according to NVQ principles. Finally, the chapter is concluded with some suggestions about where we might go from here.

PROBLEMS WITH THE NVQ PRINCIPLES

There are many publications which analyse the flaws in NVQ thinking. Perhaps most important is Hyland (1994). Others include Ashworth and Saxton (1990), Hodkinson and Issitt (1995) and Barnett (1994)[1]. Rather than revisit their varying analyses of the inherent behaviourism in NVQs, the reductionist view of learning, the naive assumptions about the relationship between theory and practice, and the lack of attention to levels of expertise, the focus here is on six fallacies that underpin the NVQ philosophy. Some of these are explicit in the NCVQ literature. Others are implicit in the ways in which the structure has developed. My purpose is to draw attention to the need to break the chains of NCVQ ideology, if we are to create a modified system of vocational qualifications that can play a part in raising the standard of VET in Britain.

Fallacy 1:   The same system and structure of vocational qualifications can or should be used in all areas of employment

The need to rationalise British vocational qualifications has already been acknowledged. However, it does not follow that the detailed system of levels, the competence focus, the tight specification of units, elements of competence, range statements and so on need to be applied with universal dogma to all occupational areas. Any successful system of VET qualifications should acknowledge that the needs of, say, retailing, engineering and social work might be significantly different. Just one of many paradoxes surrounding NVQs is the rhetoric of meeting employers' needs, whilst telling them that their needs can only be expressed in limited and rigid ways. Research is beginning to indicate that the current NVQ structure is more suitable to some occupational areas than others, and that the same competence structure may not be relevant at all to the higher levels (4 and above). Furthermore, we are already witnessing the impossibility of equating, say, a level 3 in retailing with one in engineering, despite the assumptions within the system that this must be possible.

Fallacy 2: Any job can be broken down into 'correct' component parts

Here, there are two problems. First, as Ashworth and Saxton (1990) point out, the division of competence into units and elements within the NVQ structure is unhelpfully reductionist. It falsely assumes that if all the parts are successfully achieved, the whole will also be achieved. Life is not like that. The performance of any job is holistic. To put it another way, being a plumber is partly about learning the culture of plumbing, for example relating to work-mates and understanding the ways in which plumbers behave. Brown *et al.* (1989) show that learning always entails the complex inter-relationship between context, activity and concept. Changing any one inevitably changes both the others. For example, using a chisel for a joiner is very different from the same activity for a cabinet maker. Such cultural differences, and the holistic nature of performance, cannot be reduced *entirely* to elements.

Second, even the most rigorous functional analysis results in sets of competence elements that not everyone can agree with. They are partly subjective interpretations made by, no doubt very well informed, professionals. Yet, for any job thus analysed, there are numerous other possible lists of elements that could be compiled. This would happen, for example, if slightly different criteria for an acceptable element of competence were used, or even if different people would apply current criteria differently. Senker (1995) shows that the results of functional analysis only make sense within one particular firm. Because different firms organise jobs and tasks in different ways, it is not possible to devise a uniform analysis that meets the needs of all situations. This does not mean that the carefully produced lists of elements in current NVQs are 'wrong', but it does mean that they are not exclusively right. Different versions might be more appropriate for some contexts, and if competence is to be used primarily to aid learning, the criteria for elements might be very different from those adopted by NCVQ (Hodkinson, 1992).

Fallacy 3: Competence statements can mean the same thing to all users in all situations

There are many stories of debates and confusion over the precise meanings of competence specifications within the NVQ structure. Senker (1995) reports as much in a recent survey of engineering employers. A trivial problem is that the language is off-putting and ridden with jargon. Much more importantly, we all interpret the statements in the light of our own experiences and understanding. It is impossible to tie any written text down to one universally agreed meaning. Many of you will form different interpretations of what is meant in this chapter. Yet the NVQ assessment structure is based on the false assumption that elements can possess a universal and agreed meaning. This is a more worrying cause of much of the unease about the reliability of NVQ assessments, than are claims of bias by assessors. It cannot be simply ironed out by ever more demanding verification procedures. Rather, we need an assessment system that acknowledges variations in human interpretation, in ways hinted at below.

Fallacy 4: All elements of competence can be accurately measured

This is another root cause of NVQ assessment problems. There are many reasons why many elements of competence cannot be measured with accuracy. Those who worked so hard on NVQs are aware of many of them. Indeed, part of the explanation of the burgeoning complexity of NVQs has been the need to address this problem. Assessment of any element involves a value judgement by the assessor. This can be aided by clear specifications of evidence needed and by carefully drawn up range statements, but it remains partly a value judgement. The problem, of course, is greater for some elements than for others. Dealing with this problem does not just cause greater complexity to the system. When combined with a refusal to assess anything other than each element of competence, it risks excluding from the process those parts of any job that are most difficult to measure. For example, how can we 'measure' the empathy a teacher has for her pupils? Yet many would agree that it is of central importance in doing the job. When faced with such problems, a common NVQ approach is to fall back on secondary evidence. Thus, we might be told, if the teacher has good working relationships with the children, which might be more easily 'measured', she must possess that necessary empathy. We assume that empathy contributes to good relationships, and then similarly assume that because good relationships have been measured, empathy has too. But we have no way of testing either assumption. The problems of measurement and value judgement are not unique to NVQs. The peculiar problem of NVQs is that, because the structure is entirely based in the assessment of individual elements, there is no way around the problem.

Fallacy 5: Learning is independent from performance, and the latter is derived from the former in a linear way

The NVQ framework is built on the assumption that learning and performance have a linear relationship, and that they can and should be separated. If I learn x I can then do y, and therefore if I can do y I must have learned x. Unfortunately, reality is less simple. Performance contributes to learning, so the process of training has significance in its own right – not simply as a means to achieve a specified outcome. Furthermore, it is quite possible to be able to do y without necessarily having learned x. Different people do the same tasks in different ways, and contemporary understanding about the nature of learning makes nonsense of such linear assumptions. This reminds us that NVQs fundamentally misunderstand and over-simplify the relationships between understanding and doing, and between theory and practice.

Fallacy 6: Jobs do not change, and people do not change jobs

This problem raises another paradox within NVQs. The system was designed to increase work skills in the face of rapidly changing job demands. Yet the ways in which the system has been developed only make sense if the opposite was true. This is because NVQs consist of elements of competence derived from analysing existing (past) work patterns. It is very difficult to use them to prepare trainees for jobs of the future. Furthermore, the constant need to redesignate elements as jobs do change builds in ongoing complexity and confusion to the system. The second part of the problem has two dimensions. It is difficult, within the NVQ structure, to train for a job *before* you get it. This is because there is no alternative to work-based assessment. Because separate qualifications are occupationally specific, the framework does little to encourage the development of wide-ranging understanding and abilities that would prepare people for doing new and different jobs. For these reasons, NVQs are inherently conservative, and not very well suited to a rapidly changing labour market.

THE EXPERIENCE OF NVQS WITHIN A TRAINING CREDITS PILOT SCHEME

Together with Andrew Sparkes, of Exeter University, the author conducted an investigation of one of the first Training Credits pilot schemes[2]. The details of this study have been reported elsewhere (Hodkinson and Sparkes, 1995a, b). In essence, we followed 12 young people through the first 15 months of their training process, interviewing them, their employers (18 people) and their training providers (40 people). At the time of this part of the study (September 1992 to December 1993), some trainees were using full NVQs and some were still working to NVQ equivalent qualifications. What follows are some of the conclusions we reached from this analysis about the strengths and weaknesses of NVQs, in the wider policy context of Training Credits, training markets, performance-related funding and National Training and Education Targets (NETTS).

It is clear from our study that the NVQ approach had been beneficial for many young people. David, training in agriculture, liked the fact that if he did something wrong he only had to be re-tested on that bit, rather than re-do the whole activity. His employer was also pleased with the competence elements and the system of assessment, which he felt confident about using on the farm. Similarly, Frances and her employer felt that NVQs were appropriate for retail work. Becky was struggling with a traditional type of qualification as a dental surgery assistant, and might well have been better off under an NVQ approach, which would have valued and recognised her undoubted surgery expertise, rather than assuming that her problems with written examinations accurately reflected her apparent inability to understand even basic facts.

There were suggestions in the data that NVQ approaches may be less suitable in some occupational areas than others, and less suitable for some young people than for others. For Clive, the problem lay in the need for extensive on-the-job experience that his employer could not, or would not, provide. Though working as a trainee car sales representative, his employer had insisted that he studied Business and Administration. He had attempted the NVQ level 2 but never completed it, because he could not get enough practice or evidence of business-related work in the garage. Clive himself found it difficult to understand how training built around NVQs could work. He retained a belief that the trainers he was working with should have produced a programme to give him all the training he needed, off the job. They felt unable to do this, because they could not simulate the sorts of working conditions under which NCVQ required his assessment to take place.

The concentration of training on the job, which follows from NVQ assessment procedures, created other problems. Many of the young people described gaps or weaknesses in their training programmes, because the situation where they were working did not offer the experience needed. Furthermore, the emphasis on work-based training inevitably gives employers a central, controlling role. Yet this was precisely the sort of involvement that most of the small employers we spoke to did not want. Furthermore, it meant that the training of some young people was inadequate, partly because of unhelpful employer actions. Clive's case has already been alluded to. Alison's employer was unprepared to train her in areas beyond the stables' normal activity, and Helen's first employer knew nothing of NVQs and eventually terminated her training by making her redundant. Her problem was particularly acute. Once she lost her placement, as a car body repairer, Helen's training automatically stopped as well. This was partly because of the funding regulations in the Training Credits scheme, but also because she could not get enough on-the-job experience from the college alone. Her training was wastefully cut short, though her college tutor felt that her progress had been fine.

The concentration of learning in specific workplaces creates another problem. Many of our sample of employers talked of the importance of working in their own idiosyncratic ways. This raises obvious questions. First, is such idiosyncratic training appropriate for those young people who will not be kept on in the same firm, but will look for jobs elsewhere? Second, if all trainees should be brought into contact with excellent practice, however excellence is defined, can this realistically be done in most workplaces? Third, can training in current practices prepare the adaptable and flexible workforce that current policy makers identify as essential for our future prosperity? Our interviews suggest that the answer to all of these might be 'no'. It follows that substantial elements of off-the-job training may be beneficial in most cases. This may be more necessary when a trainee is located with a small employer, even though small employers are often reluctant to release young people from the workplace.

Many of the training providers with whom we spoke felt that NVQs were not enough on their own. The agricultural college provided additional theory on David's farming course, whilst Peter's tutor, on a traditional engineering course, was highly sceptical about the adequacy of NVQs. Such views reinforce other research, which suggests that NVQs give inadequate coverage of theory and core skills. For example, Steedman and Hawkins (1994) suggest that, in the building trades, mathematical content has been greatly reduced in the transition from a traditional City and Guilds qualification to an NVQ, and that this widens the skills gap between British trainees and their counterparts in France and Germany. Our Training Credits study suggests the problem may exist in other occupational areas. A new pattern of Modern Apprenticeships is currently being piloted in Britain. This programme, which is aimed at providing high level training to young school leavers, entails a combination of NVQ, to at least level 3, with additional content. This may be a way forward for all levels of training.

NVQS AND TRAINING QUALITY

A basic assumption about the introduction of NVQs is that they will enhance the quality of VET in Britain. However, within the current British VET system, quality is emphasised but seldom defined. Gleeson and Hodkinson (1995) argue that what is understood by educational quality varies according to the beliefs of the individual. For example, within the Training Credits scheme it is unclear whether 'quality' is that which customers will buy, that which employers and the economy need, that which leads to an NVQ, or some supposedly unproblematic combination of the three.

With the current emphasis on measured achievement, educational or training quality is defined by outcomes, by far the most important of which is the achievement of a recognised qualification. Thus, under the drive to increase performance against NETTS, the qualification becomes the main determinant of quality. Especially under NVQs, it is argued that *any* programme that leads to the successful achievement of the qualification must, *ipso facto,* be quality provision and worthwhile experience. On the basis of our research evidence, that assumption must be challenged; the nature of the learning experience itself is an important part of quality, which cannot be guaranteed by the achievement of a qualification. For example, Alison had a training experience that everyone involved agreed was far from adequate. Despite this, she still succeeded in being awarded her NVQ level 2 and her training providers received their performance-related funding (Hodkinson and Hodkinson, 1995).

It is possible to draw out from the experiences in our study some elements of quality training that appear to be largely unaddressed by the current controls of markets, choice, performance-related funding and NVQ qualification. Training is an ongoing process; there is a growing body of literature about learning which recognises that it is a socio-cultural process. Brown *et al.* (1989) argue that in any learning, a combination of the learning context, the activity engaged in and the concept (or skill) being studied are dialectically interrelated. Effective learning depends on the mutual reinforcement of all three. Driver *et al.* (1994) and Cobb (1994) both talk of the importance of enculturation in learning to be a scientist or mathematician. This model of enculturation, or the gradual absorption of experience as an integral part of learning, is drawn from studies in work-based vocational contexts. Resnick (1987a) argues that the ways in which we learn in everyday life differ in significant ways from the formal approaches in schools and other learning institutions. This, of course, is the prime justification for locating the bulk of VET experience on the job. Helen was becoming a shop assistant, by absorbing the culture of the record shop where she was placed. Laura failed to become a nursery nurse because she found aspects of the work culture alienating, and left. It follows that the quality of the learning experience itself should not be overlooked.

The NVQ system does not deny the importance of a high-quality learning process, but assumes that this will inevitably be achieved from the effective specification of outputs. Unfortunately, these outputs do not directly measure the quality of the training process. One illustration of the problems caused relates to time wasting. It is widely accepted that the old apprenticeship schemes were full of 'time wasting' when, for example, trainees spent most of the first year making tea and sweeping up. Such a view ignores the possibility that young people were actually absorbing the culture of work in a useful way, which supported the technical skills they went on to develop. That old system has been replaced by one based on time saving. Programmes leading to NVQ do not specify any entitlement to training time and funding is paid partly on completion. The result is that trainers reported pressures to push young people through quickly. Despite this, many of the young people still describe time wasting. In at least some cases, this went on while gaps in the training they felt they really needed were not addressed. Time saving is, therefore, not the opposite of time wasting, as the simplistic, NCVQ view of training efficiency would seem to suggest.

Smithers (1993) and Steedman and Hawkins (1994) highlight a second problem. In the NVQ system, most assessment is done by employers or training providers in the workplace. The result is that trainers are responsible for doing the assessments, the results of which will determine whether their firm gets a substantial proportion of its funding. Steedman and Hawkins found college lecturers reporting pressure to pass weak students, and some of our interviewees said the same. In these sorts of ways, the view of training as a simple system, where the process is controlled through measuring outputs, is fundamentally flawed. As Brown and Evans (1994) claim, both processes and outcomes should receive explicit attention. To do this, a much clearer idea of what makes a quality learning process is needed, together with a policy structure that encourages the development of those features. The nature of our research only allows some tentative suggestions about what some elements of such a quality process might be.

The learning experience itself needs to be coherent and organised. Lee *et al.* (1990) criticise unstructured work experience on the Youth Training Scheme, and the use of NVQs seems to have done nothing to change that. Indeed, NVQs are designed so that assessment can be done in an *ad hoc* manner, ticking off elements of competence as they naturally occur. Furthermore, attempts by training providers to follow NVQ principles of flexibility and choice have resulted in some young people receiving disjointed off-the-job training. Steedman and Hawkins (1994) argue that all trainees should be entitled to specified amounts of off-the-job training, to address those issues not well developed in a specific workplace. It follows that the on- and off-the-job components of training need to be co-ordinated and integrated. In large firms which are responsible for both on- and off-the-job elements, this will be difficult enough. It will be even harder when small employers have to co-operate with separate training providers. The current system, which relies on negotiation in a supplier/purchaser market, has not achieved this. The employer and the training provider often have legitimate needs that are more important, to them, than achieving a coherent training programme for a young person. Alison was caught between an employer whose main concern had to be running a stables successfully, and a training provider who had to ensure that groups in college remained large enough to be viable.

Above all, a quality training process will be built around good relationships between learner, trainer and employer. Such a relationship depends, to a significant degree, on the quality of trainers being used on the scheme. Hargreaves (1994) reminds us that 'teachers don't merely deliver the curriculum. They develop, define it and reinterpret it too. It is what teachers think, what teachers believe and what teachers do ... that ultimately shapes the kind of learning young people get' (p. ix). Yet, by focusing exclusively on outcomes and assessment, NVQ dominated training schemes leave staff development of training providers unaddressed. In this, and many other senses, the retreat from the BTEC pattern of course content specification, requirements from providers of adequate resourcing and staffing, specification of criteria to control the learning process, all in addition to specification of assessment criteria, risk reducing standards, not raising them. That retreat could usefully be reversed.

USING COMPETENCE-BASED APPROACHES SUCCESSFULLY

Some interesting work on competence-based approaches has been done in youth and community work, social work and teaching, which does not accept the NVQ model in its entirety. In this section, some lessons from this sort of development work are drawn on.

Contributors to Hodkinson and Issitt (1995) reflect upon a variety of ways in which competence is currently being applied within the 'caring' professions, as well as developing a view of what competence might mean. A number of themes run through these contributions. They are interesting, because they give some pointers as to how competence-based approaches might be used effectively. The first and third of these themes in particular are explored further in Halsall's contribution in this book on core skills.

1. Holism

One strong message is that competence is a holistic concept. Training and assessment patterns need to recognise the integration of knowledge and understanding, values and skills that resides within the person who is the practitioner. As Jones (1995) shows, the personal identity of the practitioner is as important as the way she carries out her job. If it is valuable, in some ways, to disaggregate performance as a tool to aid learning and assessment, it is also vitally important to synthesise it as well. An intuitive judgement that a trainee is competent overall is as valid and important as assessments of fragmented elements of competence against performance criteria.

2. Expertise and state of the art

Competence must be seen as more than a 'can do' threshold. For competence approaches to be valuable, they must aid personal professional growth and the development of expertise. Harvard and Dunne (1995) use levels of performance within their competence scheme in teacher education to facilitate this. They write of 'state of the art', suggesting that training professionals need their practice exposed to and tested against the best practice known at the time of training. The level structure that runs through NVQs is based on a hierarchical notion of responsibilities within work, so that, for example, level 3 is equated to a supervisory role. Alternatively, Harvard and Dunne's model was devised so that increasing levels indicate increasing levels of expertise. It is important that NVQs are modified to provide incentives for trainees to become better at the tasks involved, and so that higher levels of expertise are recognised in the qualifications, for the benefit of employers and skilled workers alike.

3. Performance is not everything

Competence-based approaches can only be part of the total picture, and this is true of assessment as well as teaching and learning. Doing a job is about much more than competent performance. Above all, there is a need for higher level workers to be intellectually aware and reflectively critical, not just about their own practice but about the context in which they work, in the widest sense. This is at odds with current NVQ practice. There has to be room for negotiation around competence and its relationship to other course elements, such as knowledge, understanding, theory and developing a critical attitude.

4. A need for mentoring

Mentoring, or one-to-one tutorial support for learners, is important in a competence-based system. For a disaggregation into competence elements to aid learning, there needs to be effective dialogue between trainee and mentor. Arguably, the quality of this mentoring support is more important than the nature of the competence structures themselves. Effective mentoring may be conceived without a competence framework, but it is very hard to see competence working without effective mentoring support.

5. The importance of collaborative performance

Collaborative practice is important. In almost all work situations, success depends on working with others. In a superficial sense NVQ structures acknowledge this, for many occupational competence specifications include such factors as team work and communication. Yet there is a paradox. In a system designed on the principle that outcomes of performance are all that matters, the collaborative and collective outcomes of workers are unspecified and unmeasured. As Issitt (1995) shows, the NVQ conception is individualistic, with the built-in assumption that if each team member is competent, then their combined effect must also be competent. This flies in the face of all we know about group work and social interaction, where what one person does is deeply influenced by, and in turn influences, what others do. This is why industrial managers talk about synergy. When collaboration works well it achieves more than the sum of the parts. Not enough is known about what collaborative competence structures, which go beyond measuring individual contributions to a team, would look like.

WHITHER NVQS? PULLING THE THREADS TOGETHER

There is no attempt here to present some neat, simple summary of the implications of the preceding analysis. This is partly because I do not have a ready package of simple answers. More fundamentally, it is because one of the main reasons for the widespread inadequacies of the current system is that it was designed from just such a neat, but fatally over-simplified, approach. It began with a set of apparently straightforward principles. This grew into an increasingly complex, unwieldy and deeply flawed edifice, as the 'simple' first principles were extended and distorted to meet a combination of friendly criticism and the complexities of real life. I wish to avoid falling into a similar trap. However, a few broad issues can be identified, provided it is realised that they are problematic and that the list is incomplete.

The first is the need for pragmatic realism. The system needs to be developed in ways which recognise both complexities of education, training and employment, and the accumulated expertise of employers, training providers and others. For this reason, if no other, I disagree with those critics of NVQs who would like the whole system smashed so that we can start again. With hindsight, that is what NCVQ did to much previous practice, and the same mistake must not be made twice. Part of this pragmatic realism would be to build into the system greater variation and flexibility. Serious consideration should be given to giving NVQ accreditation to some courses that are not competence based, if that meets the needs of certain occupational sectors, certain levels of job, certain employers or even certain individual trainees. The implications of describing NVQ levels in different ways for different occupations should be explored more fully. There may well be some occupations where the NVQ framework is completely inappropriate. Apart from fundamentalist zeal and an obsession with uniformity, it is difficult to see why teacher training, for example, should be incorporated into an NVQ framework.

The next principle is about relating NVQs to broader issues of training provision and training quality. It was a grave error to separate specification of outcomes from specification of the training process. Outcome specifications, partly in the form of elements of competence, can and should be blended into broader specifications of the type familiar to anyone working with BTEC. Furthermore, outcomes based on performance can and should be combined with other outcomes, for example of understanding and knowledge. It does not have to be either/or. We can and should have both. Work from the Modern Apprenticeship pilots should be taken much further, so we can begin to decide what those other outcomes should be, with an acceptance that their nature and the balance between different types of outcome might vary from occupation to occupation and from level to level. Furthermore, the current assumptions that work-based training and assessment are the norm should be discarded. Rather, the norm should be, as in Germany, a mixture of on- and off-the-job training, the balance between the two determined according to occupational needs and particular circumstances. At least for trainees embarking on a new job or career, an entitlement to minimum training time, both on and off the job, should be introduced. This is needed for enculturation. If some trainees progress very quickly, the extra time can be used to raise their levels of expertise.

There should also be a much more varied approach to assessment within the system. It is a truism that all assessments are imperfect and value laden. It follows that a multi-stranded assessment approach has a greater chance of being both valid and reliable. NCVQ recognise this in the breadth of evidence that is acceptable to demonstrate that the performance criteria have been met. The problem is that other forms of assessment, that are not directly related to elements of competence in the workplace, are virtually excluded. There may well be a place, in some schemes, for holistic judgements about performance, practical and written tests, practical and written assignments or 'projects', etc.

Finally, the place of general education within vocational qualifications needs to be seriously considered. Our European partners would assume that this was a normal and essential part of training programmes at all levels (Green, 1995). The current fashionable approach to core skills is a pitiably narrow and reductionist version of what is needed. As Resnick (1987a) suggests, it is the broad-based benefits of an appropriate general education that are most likely to prepare young people (and others) for life in a rapidly changing world, where the skills of any particular job or workplace may become rapidly obsolete. Exactly what such a general vocational education should consist of is currently unclear.

As with the other points raised in this chapter, more thinking and research are required. In the meantime, let us move forward pragmatically, and discard the fundamentalist baggage of inappropriate NVQ principles, whilst avoiding the temptation to replace them with others. Above all, we need to free up the gains made within the NVQ framework, whilst beginning to address seriously the rather more numerous weaknesses.

NOTES

1. Readings which are more favourably inclined to the NVQ position include Black and Wolf (1990), Burke (1989, 1995) and Jessup (1991), together with the considerable output from the NCVQ and from the Standards Branch of the Employment Department.
2. Training Credits are vouchers, to be spent by young people on training leading to NVQ qualifications, within Youth Training regulations. They have been piloted since 1991, and became national from September 1995. The study was funded by the Economic and Social Research Council (ESRC) and I am grateful for their support.

4

Vocationalism and Vocational Courses 14–16

Mike Cockett

INTRODUCTION

The word 'vocationalism' does not appear in the dictionaries as yet but it has made an appearance in recent literature discussing developments in work-related education and training (Dale, 1985). Because it is a new word, some definition and justification may be offered for its use. The rise in the importance of vocational education and training has been well documented, in this book as elsewhere (e.g. Hodkinson and Issit, 1995). The causes are also largely agreed, being based on the 'post Fordist' analysis of the need of industry for a flexible, well-trained work-force whose members expect to re-train for their next job just as they are expected to be well-trained for their current one. Indeed, this analysis is so all pervading that while there might be disagreements on the means of delivering this well-trained and well-motivated work force, and even on whether it is possible in this country, the desirability, and the need to do so is taken by the vast majority as axiomatic.

For the purposes of this chapter, 'vocationalism' is taken to be a belief in the value of vocational education and training and it has a long, though not undisputed, history. The term 'new vocationalism', coined to describe the renewed interest in and drive towards, what is seen as, greater vocational relevance in the curriculum both pre- and post-16, implies such a history. Coffey (1992) traces the division of education into the general, often called liberal, on the one hand and the vocational or utilitarian on the other, back to classical Greece. He also illustrates the cyclical nature of the process in two respects. First, the vocational curriculum of one age becomes the liberal general curriculum of another as with the classics, originally regarded as vocational courses for future clerics but later the sign of the liberally educated man. Second, he shows how the rise and fall of concern about the vocational relevance of the curriculum is linked to the fall and rise of economic prosperity.

In one important sense, as Coffey illustrates, it is not possible to avoid the vocational significance of the curriculum, especially where there are perceived differences in status between different curricula. Latin and Greek may not have been directly vocationally relevant in the nineteenth century but a man with Latin and Greek, by demonstrating thus his class and culture, had access to the higher professions. This is the current paradox. The courses giving the broadest range of vocational access are the academic courses. Vocational courses narrow choice and, at the lower levels, may never lead to actual employment (Gleeson, 1990; Spours and Young, 1990).

It is possible to take a political perspective on this current manifestation of vocationalism as Gleeson (1990) does, arguing that a major purpose behind the development of vocational options in schools, Youth Training initiatives and the Technical and Vocational Education Initiative (TVEI) is the supply of a workforce conditioned to the needs of industry and, further, that the purpose of some programmes, particularly the Youth Training Scheme, was more to hide youth unemployment than to provide the highly skilled and flexible work-force which industry supposedly was demanding. However, the purpose of this chapter is narrower in that it examines some of the mechanisms in schools and the communities they serve which operate against vocational courses and vocational elements in courses. It will be argued that it is because these issues have not been addressed, that past attempts to introduce such courses have failed and that future attempts will also be blighted. The main focus is the fate of various special measures taken to deal with those pupils who are failing in the mainstream provision, though there will also be reference to those measures aimed at providing a vocational element in the curriculum for all pupils.

The assumption of the chapter is that there is nothing wrong with a relationship between work and education (Spours and Young, 1990). Indeed, it is taken as axiomatic that a major purpose of schooling is to prepare pupils for adult and working life and that this cannot be done without also recognising the needs of society in general and industry in particular. The argument is about how this is best done. Is it, as some would argue, to be achieved through making the curriculum 'vocationally relevant' (Prime Minister Callaghan's Ruskin College Speech, 1976; Jones, 1989), or is it by providing a truly comprehensive liberal education (Holt and Reid, 1988)? Whatever is to be attempted, it should take account of past efforts to achieve just such a relationship at least for some of the pupils some of the time.

This is not the first time these issues have been addressed (e.g. Pollard *et al.*, 1988) but since, with the introduction of part one General National Vocational Qualifications (GNVQs) into the school curriculum, we seem to be travelling, if not the same, then a similar route, it is worth spelling out why it was that previous initiatives, however lauded they were at the time, have left us with exactly the same problems to solve. Here, I wish to declare an interest. I started teaching in 1963, the year the Newsom Report was published and I have, since 1982, been first a co-ordinator of a Lower Attaining Pupils Project (LAPP) and later a TVEI co-ordinator. In addition, the LAPP project was part of the EEC Transition from School to Adult and Working Life project (Transition II). It is necessary to declare this because the following commentary is based largely on that experience.

HALF OUR FUTURE

The Newsom Report of the Central Advisory Council For Education (DES, 1963) is a useful starting point because its title, *Half Our Future*, is suggestive of one of the major problems confronting us today. The terms of reference of the Council were:

> to consider the education between the ages of 13 and 16 of pupils of average or less than average ability who are or will be following full time courses either at schools or in establishments of further education. The term education shall be understood to include extra-curricular activities (p.xv).

Previously, the Crowther Report (Ministry of Education, 1959) had proposed the raising of the school leaving age to 16 and the Newsom Report endorsed that proposal. It is tempting to reproduce the whole of the introduction to the report if only for its historical interest. What report these days would contain the statement, 'We make no apologies for recommendations which will involve an increase in public expenditure on the education of the average pupils' (p.xiv)? In summary, Newsom's solution to the problem of educating the average and below average was to provide good teaching, in good accommodation of an appropriate curriculum to relatively small groups of boys and girls. The economic importance of addressing the needs of this group was acknowledged, but the general tenor of the recommendations was based on a general/liberal notion of education (Moore, 1990). Thus:

> Their future role politically, socially and economically is vital to our national life but, even more important, each is an individual whose spirit needs education as much as his body needs nourishment. Without adequate education human life is impoverished (DES, 1963: xiv).

When the school-leaving age was raised in 1972 there were serious attempts to follow this prescription. Many authorities built new units (the RoSLA units) which embodied the Newsom proposals for flexible spaces, practical areas, social areas and classrooms clearly designed for small groups. There were attempts to provide a curriculum which, in Newsom's terms, was practical, realistic, vocational and which offered some choice about what they should learn. The term vocational, 'a dangerous but indispensable word' (DES, 1963: para. 322) needed some explanation. In the currency of the time it implied a *calling*, for example, to be a priest, and Newsom was aware of the anomaly of using the same term to describe a course in bricklaying. But, it was thought, the humble starting point of a simple practical course could lead to a greater commitment to learning in general: 'They know that shop assistants, for instance, have to talk to customers; and with this knowledge the whole of English, not just some special limited "trade English", gains significance' (DES, 1963: para. 322).

The point I wish to make here is not that the Newsom Report is embedded in the social and political context of the time, which it is, but that it makes exactly the same assumptions about what will motivate young people which are behind all the initiatives, including part one GNVQs, aimed at providing a suitable education for half our school population. The heart of the Newsom argument, in spite of reservations about the reduction in manual work, is that many of the average and below average 'will work with their hands' (DES, 1963: para. 324) and that practical, vocational courses or aspects of courses will be valued because 'it may be school, but it is also real' (DES, 1963: para. 324). The average and below average pupils, it is maintained, will be motivated to learn because of these 'real world' links. Even at the time there was a tension between the fine phrases of the report and the perceptions of teachers about what was possible. Teachers struggling with the 'fourth year leavers' were not convinced by the exhortations to use 'animal husbandry, brickwork, and cement work, drainage, fencing, estate maintenance, the erection of useful constructions in the service of the school' (Newsom, 1963: para. 383) as the context for general education or that the 'domestic crafts' would be motivating because 'they are recognisably part of adult living' and because 'girls know that whether they marry early or not, they are likely to find themselves eventually making and running a home' (Newsom, 1963: para. 388).

Nevertheless, serious attempts were made to implement the spirit if not the detailed prescriptions of the report. When the school-leaving age was raised in 1972–73 there was a proliferation of mode 3 CSE courses, some of them limited grade courses aimed at this new group of pupils. The courses were often backed by resources both in materials and teacher time. So what happened to them and why, if the answer is to provide relevance through vocationally oriented courses, do we still have the problem of disaffected, less able pupils?

LOWER ATTAINING PUPILS PROJECT (LAPP)

Sir Keith Joseph, then Secretary of State for Education, set up LAPP in 1982. He was not concerned with quite half our future but with the 'bottom forty per cent'. One argument (Burgess, 1988) is that the programmes for lower attaining pupils were very largely Newsom revisited, though others claimed that LAPP was a step backwards, the divisive effects of the Newsom proposals having been recognised and newer more inclusive courses having, in the meantime, been developed.

In fact, while many participants in the scheme reported a sense of *déjà vu* (Weston, 1988), in most, though not all programmes, there was some attempt at least to blur the distinction between courses for the 'less able' and the mainstream curriculum of the school. The courses would appear in the option scheme and technically be available to all abilities. Some schemes offered an 'alternative' programme for a small part of the week to all pupils and some promoted cross-curricular programmes potentially as valuable to the most able as well as to the least able, for example in 'thinking skills' or 'oracy'.

According to the national evaluation of the project (Weston, 1988)

LAPP was to be distinguished from previous programmes, first because it was a national project and second, because it addressed two issues, attainment and differentiation, which, supposedly, had not been addressed before or at least not with the same focus. It has to be said that, for those running the projects, this was not obvious in the first instance. It was only gradually that this agenda emerged. Attainment was to be tackled both in terms of raising attainment in core areas such as English and mathematics but also, to an extent, in redefining attainment to include areas in which the least able were thought likely to be able to achieve something recognisable. Differentiation was to be achieved by recognising which pupils were suited to which curriculum and was an attack on the perceived effects of egalitarian policies which would not differentiate, on the grounds that it discriminated between pupils. This, it was claimed, condemned large numbers of them to a curriculum which was unsuited to their abilities. The bright were held back, the less able bemused.

One scheme was titled the Alternative Curriculum Strategies Project with the clear signal that the problem was the unsuitability of the curriculum and that, once the right curriculum had been found, the lower attainers and the disaffected would be re-engaged with education. In fact, in spite of the great energy and inventiveness which went into developing alternatives to the standard curriculum the old notions of school attainment prevailed. As Weston reported:

> In practice it has proved hard for many teachers (and indeed pupils) to shift from long established presuppositions about the kind of attainment that schools value – and related judgments about pupils and what can be expected of them. (Weston, 1988:6)

and again,

> Like teachers, pupils found it difficult to rethink their ideas about attainment and what counted as real work. For some, real work at school meant writing … and getting real marks even if they were discouraging. (Weston, 1988:13; see also Hustler et al., 1991).

It would be untrue to say that LAPP had no impact. Some of the ideas and outcomes did have an effect, at least for a time, on the way teachers thought about their pupils and the quality of their relationships with them. It would also be untrue to say that the curriculum itself did not interest the pupils. There were many examples of individuals and groups who seemed transformed for a time both in their attitudes and in their 'alternative' attainments. The effort to see all attainment in a positive light, as opposed to the implied negative of comparative grades, influenced the development of Records of Achievement. Last, but by no means least, schools which ran successful alternative programmes felt the benefit for all pupils, in that the mainstream curriculum ran more smoothly without the typically disruptive presence of the 'lower attainers' (Weston, 1988). But for all that, the project did not solve the problem of the 'bottom forty per cent'.

TVEI AND COMPACTS

TVEI was set up at the same time as LAPP and with relatively massive resources in the 14, first-phase, pilot authorities. It was not intended to be a programme for lower attainers but, because it was an alternative programme, the first cohorts were in fact largely taken from that group. Steps were taken to avoid this in later phase pilots, with mixed success, but the problem was not overcome until the extension programme directly involved all pupils and TVEI sponsored GCSE courses came on stream. The nature of these courses and their fate will be discussed later; for the moment the focus is on the development of Compacts which, being promoted by the Training Agency, were under the same umbrella as TVEI and, indeed, were often set up by TVEI staff within local authorities.

Compacts had their origin in programmes developed in Boston, USA and were based originally on the simple premise that industry could expect certain things of education, but in return, education could expect a response from industry, in particular, jobs for students who achieved their Compact goals. In that form, Compacts were based on the now familiar argument that the key to the motivation of young people lay in there being clear vocational outcomes. Engagement in the school curriculum was encouraged, not so much by the intrinsic interest or value of the curriculum itself, but by the promise of the job prize at the end. In return, schools would adapt the curriculum to meet the perceived needs of employers. This simple model was never attempted in the UK and was soon modified in Boston but the notion of a 'deal' remains (Hartley, 1992). The *Compacts Development Handbook* (Training Agency, 1988) extends the employer commitment to the support of young people through further and higher education as well as the more direct offer of jobs. There is at least in theory, a concern to support all pupils. However, in practice Compacts support the same lower attainers that concerned Sir Keith Joseph. (In the beginning, in fact, they were specifically inner city initiatives.) They represent an alternative to success in the mainstream and, through the promotion of such things as work experience, mini-enterprise, careers talks and mock interviews, offer at least some aspects of an alternative curriculum.

We will never know if Compacts in their original form which included job guarantees would have worked more effectively than they did. In the event the downturn in the economy intervened and few employers would make such a commitment. The jobs guarantee was soon reduced to a chance at any new jobs which came available through a guaranteed job interview and although employers continue to be involved in various education industry programmes, the 'deal' from the pupils' point of view is now little more than the old promise that if they improve their employment related skills they will have a better chance of being employed. The only 'guarantee' they are left with is that of a place on a post-16 course which they can get whether or not they meet their Compact goals.

GENERAL NATIONAL VOCATIONAL QUALIFICATIONS

At the time of writing the GNVQ part one programme offering units towards GNVQ qualification from the age of 14 is about to begin in selected pilot schools. The rhetoric surrounding GNVQ is that it is an alternative qualification to A-levels or to GCSE depending on the level at which it is taken. The vocational purpose of the qualification is contained in the title and in the pilot programmes the examination boards are at pains to stress the need for the qualification to be seen as an alternative across the ability range. The last thing the National Council for Vocational Qualifications wants is for GNVQ to become the lower attainer's certificate.

Of course, with each new attempt to use the vocational, real world scenario to motivate young people to greater educational attainment there is some new slant, some hoped for improvement, and it would be unnecessarily cynical to claim that none of these could ever be successful. In the case of GNVQ there is the possibility, at least in theory, that students starting at the lowest levels of the GNVQ ladder can progress to university entrance level and that, since there are already students at university on the basis of their GNVQs, this is not an idle promise. This is by no means an insignificant development and, all other things being equal, might benefit at least some of the average and below average pupils. There are already signs post-16 (FEU, 1994; and Chapter 5) that students see GNVQs as preferable to repeat GCSEs and either as a complement, or an alternative, to A-levels.

Putting on one side, for the time being, arguments about the value of a specifically vocational approach to the curriculum pre-16, the argument is exactly the same as with post-16. If the qualification is to have any chance of reaching parity of esteem, then it must be seen as being available to all pupils. This notion has been killed at the outset by the Schools Curriculum and Assessment Authority. Dr Nick Tate, the Council's Chief Executive, stated that 'Some schools will choose not to offer vocational courses pre-16. ... Even more schools will choose to keep vocational courses as an optional, rather than compulsory, element within the key stage 4 curriculum' (*TES*, 31 March 1995). This was interpreted by one headteacher as meaning 'If you've got a bright A-level kid, they don't have to go down that road, do they?' GNVQ part one is not designed for low attainers but it shares some of the problems of Newsom and LAPP courses. It cuts across the normal organisation of schools; it is expensive in time and resources; although it may avoid the fate of being a lower attainers' certificate, it is unlikely to attract the most able and, although there is some built-in progression, as long as pupils stay on the chosen GNVQ course route (which is to be welcomed) there is still much uncertainty about transfer from one GNVQ to another and from GNVQ to other qualifications post-16.

WHY THE NEW 'VOCATIONAL' CURRICULUM WILL FAIL

As referred to earlier, there are strong, political and social arguments advanced against the New Vocationalism. My position, though in some ways more pragmatic, reaches much the same conclusion. It may be that in an ideal world we should be offering a broad, balanced, liberal and thus liberating curriculum to all pupils. The problem is, we are faced with the classic chicken and egg situation.

Concern for, and the freedom to pursue, a liberal education (increasingly any sort of education) is dependent on a level of economic prosperity both for the nation as a whole and for individual families. That economic prosperity, so we are told, is itself dependent on an improved level of education and training which typically is not available to those at the lower levels of the economy. The fact is that any way of breaking that cycle is worth a try. If some Compact graduates get jobs, however vocationally narrow their options will seem to have been, there is at least the chance, particularly if the job is with training, that they can work their way out of both the educational and the economic poverty traps. The failure of past and present and, from all indications, future attempts to provide a curriculum suited to the needs of lower attainers whether we regard that as 40% or 50% of the school population lies not in a failure to produce alternative curricula nor in terms of the political or cultural issues, though these are major factors. It is rooted in bad psychology.

When I was the project leader for one of the Lower Attaining Pupils projects I was often asked to talk to teachers and others about the project and the pupils involved in it. It seemed to me important at the time to try to give the 'audience' for these sessions some impression of what it was like to be a lower attainer. On one occasion, perhaps because of my own insecurities in this area, I decided that many of the audience would feel insecure about their talents as artists. My method was first to ask for someone in the audience to volunteer that they had some artistic ability. This was not always easy, but someone was always identified. The audience were then told that this person was going to assess their attempts at drawing a portrait of some other person in the room. At the end of a set period of time they would put their names on the paper and hand them in for assessment. The assessor was to place the drawing in three piles. The first was of those with artistic talent, the second those who had some idea but were not particularly gifted, the third was for those with no artistic talent.

Originally, the exercise was designed to give some of the audience the sensation of being asked to do something in a very public way which they knew they could not do. It succeeded in this and in much more. The teachers and initial teacher training students who were the victims of this strategy displayed a range of behaviours, some of which were constant across all the groups (perhaps 10 or 15 in all) and some of which were more occasional. In all groups significant numbers worked hard at the exercise, clearly trying to do their best to produce an effective portrait. All groups had jokers who made fun of the exercise both by calling out to others in the group and by producing joke pictures. Often they were actively disruptive, passing comments on other people's efforts, for example. A favourite ploy was deliberately to produce obviously childish drawings. Frequently, there were dropouts who refused to do the exercise saying it was stupid and that they had not come along to play games. Occasionally, people became very upset and on one occasion two people walked out of the session, one of them in tears.

Once handed in, the drawings were assessed and placed in piles in front of the group. I picked up the lowest rated pile and asked people to say whether they thought they would find their drawing in it. In spite of the fact that it was usually the smallest pile, large numbers claimed that they expected to find themselves there. This then was the basis for a discussion about the feelings involved and the behaviour displayed by the group. In brief, they produced most of the behaviours which, if persistent, would have identified them as candidates for a lower attainers programme. A final twist was to ask some of the 'low attainers' how they would feel if all in service training sessions involved drawing and if their careers depended on it.

Enough has been said to make the point. Lower attainers are not beings from a parallel universe. If you prick them they bleed. Like the teachers in the exercise, they are lower attainers because the context defines them as such and, like the teachers, they respond by challenging the value of that context, by dropping out and sometimes by getting deeply upset. But, also like the teachers, they were 'hooked' by the system. Given the chance, they wanted success as defined by the context, not as defined by some alternative, however attractive that might be. There is one touching postscript to the exercise. Although I deliberately did not list which drawings had ended up in which pile, many teachers, at the end of the session, wanted to know what assessment they had been given. This is not a joke at their expense; it is an illustration of the way we are. The point is, that the provision of an alternative curriculum, whether it is a Newsom course, a LAPP course or GNVQ part 1, does not change the context. However intrinsically interesting the course, you are still in the bottom pile.

The fate of all curricula aimed specifically at the needs of lower attainers follows an established pattern. There is a period of development and commitment during which the special courses recruit both effective teachers and significant numbers of pupils. There is a period of establishment during which participation in that curriculum marks the pupils and the teachers as lower attainers and there is a period of decline as the pioneering teachers withdraw, often pleading exhaustion, and parents and pupils refuse to opt for courses which mark them as less able. Evans and Davies (1988) describe a particularly stark example of this process in which two courses, in one school, supposedly relevant to the less able because they were both practical and vocational, recruited well in the first year but failed to recruit in the second. The decline of the courses is based on a number of factors and it is worth considering these in some detail since any proposed solutions to the problems posed here must take them into account.

The question of status

Raffe (1985) raises this issue in discussing the problem of attempting curriculum reform from the bottom up:

> Courses introduced at the bottom of the educational ladder acquire low status, and their students become stigmatised by employers and educational selectors as the less able. The motivation of those on the courses suffers. Abler and 'better motivated' students are reluctant to enter the courses lest they too be stigmatised and lose their position in the educational (and subsequently occupational) hierarchy. A vicious circle is thus created, and the net result of introducing educational reforms in this way might be merely to reinforce existing biases within education, by conveying the message that the new approaches are only relevant to those who lack ability or the motivation to try something better. (Raffe, 1985: 20–21)

Whatever the quality of the course, it tends to take on the status of the pupils recruited to it and, whoever else might be recruited, forces within schools ensure that it includes the least able and most disruptive individuals. Under LAPP few schools managed to recruit anything like 40% of their intake to the courses (Weston, 1988) and in some it was as little as 10 or 15%. In the early stages pupils and their parents believe the rhetoric surrounding the new courses. They may have low academic attainments but they are not stupid. They recognise that they may be better off following some other path than the one on which they were currently stumbling. Within a very short space of time, however, recruitment becomes negative. Pupils not coping in mainstream courses are told they should be in the alternative and this includes disruptive and truanting pupils. The point has been made earlier that disaffection and consequent disruptive behaviour is, in part, the result of an unsuitable curriculum. Unfortunately, certainly by Year 10, the behaviour continues even when the curriculum is changed and soon the alternative group becomes characterised by deviant behaviour rather than by the curriculum they are following. Future potential recruits and their parents reject the option because they do not wish to be characterised in that way.

Courses which are based on some sort of 'vocational' promise, that they will prepare the pupils for the world of work face a further difficulty. There is no vocational advantage in following such a course since employers will recruit what they see to be the best available students and their measure for this continues to be examination success. Raffe (1985) suggests this is because employers avoid taking risks and are anyway not likely to be well informed about new developments in education. Williams (1994) suggests that in any case employers want recruits with a good general education and are not interested in them being already trained with specific skills. There is a similar hierarchy in post-16 college recruitment. Courses divide broadly into two groups, those which require GCSEs at grade C and above and those which do not. For those which do not, entry may be on the basis of 'a good general education', a record of achievement and an interview. The problem in establishing vocational courses pre-16 is not some mass rejection of the culture of the school but, on the contrary, a mass acceptance of the culture of schooling and the criteria established through examination and selection procedures for defining success and failure.

Timetables and cultures

Almost all attempts to develop new courses, whether with the broadly liberal intent of Newsom or the more directly vocational GNVQ involve new ways of managing school time. The importance of this issue cannot be over-estimated. It has consequences both for the courses themselves and for the teachers teaching them. The timetable dictates the use of school time. With few exceptions it slices up the week into time slots which remain unchanged throughout the year. It is designed for the delivery of separate independent subjects and it is jealously guarded by school staff. Subject teachers manage their teaching to fit the time slots available. Departments bargain for what they see as their rightful slice of the week and senior management see adherence to the timetable as the key to social control.

Practical subjects have always presented a problem because the logistics of managing practical activities demand larger blocks of time. In addition, the practical subjects were often stereotyped as 'boys and girls' activities and the attempt to avoid stereotyping effectively added a number of subjects to the curriculum, a problem not yet solved by National Curriculum technology. The resulting carousels of technology courses were an uneasy compromise. New courses at 14+ add a new dimension. Not only do they need larger blocks of time, but the time needed varies across the year to accommodate such things as link courses with colleges, project work and work experience. One of the advantages of the LAPP groups which were timetabled separately was that the team of teachers who taught them could co-ordinate their use of time. This is a pattern familiar in vocational courses post-16 but it is counter to school culture and organisation. The effect is that, for those teachers heavily involved in the low attainers curriculum, it is almost impossible for them to have any other significant teaching role. The alternative curriculum becomes their teaching life with the consequence that they spend most of their time dealing with the most difficult pupils in the school. It is equally difficult to involve teachers whose major commitment is not the alternative course and the course will be staffed for some of the time not by teachers who are committed to the course and involved in developing it, but by those who, by accident of timetabling, happen to be available.

There have been some half-way solutions attempted, with the 'alternative' course covering more than one option group and for the choice of that option to dictate, for example, English and mathematics groupings. This seems to be the preferred GNVQ part one model. It does make more time per week available but it makes it more difficult to establish a course team and whole course planning. Technically, the slimmed down National Curriculum and the less prescriptive programme at Key Stage 4 does allow more flexibility (Dearing, 1993) but the core problem remains and that is tension between single-subject and whole-course management. A further source of tension is in the resources which alternative courses demand. They are more expensive than most mainstream courses, both in materials and in teacher time. In the pilot stages when the courses were externally funded, there was great resentment that extra resources were being spent on pupils who seemed to be the least worthy. The effects of these tensions on teachers of alternative courses is that they become exhausted, both through dealing with the social and behavioural problems which they inherit and because they are constantly needing alterations to school organisation either permanently or temporary. They need to work with cross-curricular teams and they need to co-ordinate work across more than one subject area, all of which run counter to prevailing school organisation. The effect of the exhaustion is that many ask to re-enter the mainstream of the school or they apply for jobs elsewhere. The loss of the pioneering teachers is often the final blow to the alternative course.

WHOLE SCHOOL DEVELOPMENTS

Whilst the main thrust of this chapter is a consideration of separate courses for low attainers, something needs to be said about developments, especially in the field of the work-related curriculum, which are intended for all pupils. There is insufficient space here to consider the development of TVEI in detail but many of the problems described above were recognised in that initiative and as pilot phase moved to extension phase the emphasis on a separate target group disappeared and authorities, schools and colleges had to show how the extension programme would apply to all pupils. Initially there was considerable success. Work experience became almost universal, Records of Achievement were given statutory status and many TVEI-sponsored GCSE courses proved popular. TVEI seemed to have affected the ways teachers thought about their work, not only in terms of a work-related curriculum content but in terms of methodologies, including negotiated learning, problem solving and active learning which were seen to be an appropriate preparation for a flexible, creative work-force (Saunders and Halpin, 1990). However, the National Curriculum only paid lip service to TVEI and in subsequent developments many of the TVEI-promoted programmes were nullified by, for example, the move against modular courses and the restriction on course work. Lawton (1994) traces the process by which what were seen as the old values were re-established. The process has placed in jeopardy virtually all TVEI developments. The status of those GCSEs largely based on course work is reduced, the value of balanced science is questioned, time for work experience and problem solving practical work is squeezed. The pressure to succeed in producing the maximum possible output of high grades is already squeezing vocational elements out. The instrumental value placed on five grade Cs and above endangers not only vocational courses for the less able but the vocational aspects of all courses.

SOLUTIONS?

Of course, there are difficulties in solving these problems, not least because the conditions for change depend on factors, especially economic factors, beyond the control of schools and the education system (Young, 1993a). On the other hand, it is possible to learn from the past and, at least, to minimise negative, and maximise positive, factors. In doing so we will have to face up to the dilemmas which this chapter has illustrated and in order to learn we need to act. Certainly, the National Curriculum has not proved to be a curriculum for all pupils. Its subject structure and its associated testing and assessment arrangements impose an organisation on schools which precludes a flexible response to the needs of pupils. It discourages co-operation between subject departments and sets them in competition with each other for good grades and for the time and the resources they feel they need to produce them (Hargeaves, 1994).

The first action that might be taken would be to reduce this isolationism and to develop more flexible co-operative responses to the various needs of all pupils. Co-operation would involve a willingness to manage time more flexibly, a willingness to pursue the vocational aspects of the curriculum for all pupils and an attempt to develop methods of 'whole course management' which reduce the emphasis on individual grades and increase the emphasis on breadth and balance.

The second action follows from the first and would be to increase the ways in which achievement can be seen as multifaceted and progressive (Finegold et al., 1990). This may mean, at least as an interim measure, co-operating with local colleges to increase the recognition of the value of grades below C. The offer of an alternative, vocational, curriculum to those who are not expected to be academic successes is based on the false premise that it is possible to differentiate between the vocational and academic pupils (Lawton, 1994) and that pupils and their parents will accept that categorisation. It is a categorisation reinforced by the introduction of GNVQ part one. One of the ironies of current policies is that the emphasis on parental choice makes the acceptance of this division even less likely. This is not simply a problem in the UK. All industrialised countries have some division of this sort (Young, 1993b). The reason why the system is under question is not because there is a need for greater vocational relevance in the curriculum but that the reduced need for manual labour makes the old vocational pathways irrelevant. Ironically, the 'real world', practical course of Newsom and LAPP and of other such programmes is increasingly unreal. Whatever industry wants it is not young people coming through with the level of skill in manual trades which schools might provide (Williams, 1994).

This leads to the third action which is to further the debate, not about how we make the curriculum relevant, but about what we mean by relevance (Hodkinson, 1991; Spours and Young, 1990; Young, 1993a). Newsom took it to mean being related to jobs which pupils could see around them. They would be motivated because learning job-related skills would be a mark of growing up. The radical changes in work and family life since then have made such reasoning redundant. On the other hand, and this is the paradox with which we have to struggle, the falling opportunities for 'real' work for young people places a greater responsibility on the education system to prepare their students for whatever may come their way. Relevance for an unpredictable and uncertain future is not so easy to define. Whatever we come up with it will have to be a definition which is applied to all pupils.

5

Caught in the Middle – Transition at 16+

Mike Cockett and John Callaghan

INTRODUCTION

There have been many calls recently for changes to the system of awards offered to young people from 14+ onwards (Finegold *et al.*, 1990; National Commission on Education, 1993; Spours, 1992; and Chapter 2). These arise from an understanding that the current system is confusing, divisive and consequently demotivating. The drive behind these calls comes from various sources. A modernisation of academic and vocational qualifications is seen as essential to the industrial needs of the nation (White Papers, 1994, 1995). The divide between academic and vocational, whilst historically of long standing (Coffey, 1992) is seen as an historical anachronism (Green, 1993) and one which must be overcome (Spours and Young, 1990). There are pedagogic objections to seeing academic and vocational learning as fundamentally different and there are claims that the instrumental use of qualifications chiefly as a selective mechanism for higher level courses and ultimately higher education is counter-productive (Lawton, 1994).

The interim report on education and training from Sir Ron Dearing (1995) looks forward to a coherent, overarching framework for qualifications at 16+. This has been broadly welcomed and there is even the hope that the introduction of such a framework will not become a political issue. It will, however, take time and especially, as the report admits, it will take time for such a framework to be understood and accepted. For the time being the 'culture of lifetime learning' must be envisaged in the context of current provision where the only major new development is the introduction of GNVQs. Although this study of transition at 16+ was undertaken before a review of post-16 qualifications was even proposed, we believe that the issues raised are highly relevant to the development of a new framework.

The popularity of GNVQs has taken even their designers by surprise and the reasons for this popularity are not yet apparent. What is clear is that, although GNVQs were untried, especially in some of their more ambitious aspirations (to be an alternative to A-levels and to provide access to higher education), they recruited heavily as soon as they were made available. We might assume from this that there was already an unsatisfied need for alternative courses for certain groups of students. Even the untried GNVQ, it would appear, is seen as being better than the mixture of vocational courses, A-levels and repeat GCSEs on offer up until that time.

Although some students have chosen to follow a GNVQ course when they could have taken A-levels, the majority have chosen them as an alternative to repeating GCSE courses or more specific vocational courses at levels 1 or 2.[1] This study is focused on students who have, on the whole, just failed to reach A-level entry standards which are broadly the same as entry to Advanced GNVQ and NVQ level 3 courses. The argument is that it is precisely this group of students who are crucial to the success of policies aimed at raising standards generally and in promoting a positive attitude to a continuity of education and training. The purpose of the research, on which this chapter is based, was to provide an insight into the perceptions and attitudes of a group of young people who had just made the transition from school to college and who were following courses where entry requirements were less than four GCSEs at grade C.

RESEARCH OUTLINE

A total of 37 students were interviewed from four different colleges, two sixth form and two further education, in four local authority areas in Greater Manchester. Between them they were following 14 courses, the vast majority being GNVQ Intermediate or NVQ level 2 courses. Some were repeating GCSE courses and some were doing a mixture of the two. The original intention was that all the interviewees would have left school the previous year but in the event a number of older students were also interviewed. Whilst these older students provided an interesting perspective on the process of transition, some of them having made several transitions, their perceptions of school and college did not differ radically from those of the younger students. In one college two GNVQ advanced level students were also interviewed and again this provided a perspective for the researchers but the number was too small for any comparative claims to be made.

Two interview methods were used, individual interviews and group interviews/discussions. In both cases students were asked to describe their current course and their ambitions, to reflect on how they ended up on that course, to talk about their final year at school and their GCSE results and to make some overall assessment of what they felt they had gained from their schooling. They were all interviewed towards the middle of the first term of their new courses and their responses represent what they were thinking at that time. This is a limitation on the research. We do not know how their ideas changed over the period of transition from school to college and we do not know how their ideas have changed as they have moved further into their new courses.

All interviews were transcribed, including group discussions and they were examined for a number of themes. Where possible, individual responses were identified. Whilst the same issues were covered in the group interviews as in the individual interviews the responses varied, often centring on differences between schools. In addition not all areas on which there was consensus are apparent from the transcriptions because assent was sometimes non-verbal and could not be included in the frequency counts.

Thirty five of the interviewees came from seven different NVQ level 2 and GNVQ intermediate level courses with entry requirements of less than four GCSEs at grade C or above. Two were following GNVQ advanced courses with a notional entry requirement of four GCSEs at grade C or above. This weighting was a deliberate choice. The young people entering the level 2 or intermediate courses are drawn from the largest group of young people leaving school. (In the four LEA areas represented, the percentage of young people leaving with less than five grade C and above ranged from 59% to 76%.)

All the students interviewed had achieved at least one GCSE grade G or above and 25 had grade C in at least one subject with other grades ranging from grades G to D. The group is most easily characterised against the normal entry requirements for A-level or advanced GNVQ. For these levels only Grade C and above are accepted as qualifying grades. Table 5.1 shows the spread of GCSE of grade C and above.

Table 5.1

	No. grade C or above GCSEs	1–>3 grade C or above GCSEs	4 grade C or above GCSEs	Total
Sixth form college	4	7	3	14
FE	8	11	4	23

A BROAD ANALYSIS OF THE RESULTS

The interviews were analysed under four broad headings: attitudes to achievements including achievements in mathematics and English, the value placed on GCSE grades, references to personal motivation in relation to their past and current courses and references to the process of transition.

Students were asked to comment on their attitudes to school achievements both in general terms and with specific reference to their results at GCSE; 12 positive and 26 negative responses were obtained relating to their results (some students gave both positive and negative responses). Typically, they were positive about grades C and above and negative about grades below C. All the students made reference to 'passing GCSE'. This will be discussed in detail later. We were careful not to introduce this notion in the questions asked and the students were asked to explain when they used the phrase. In all cases they considered a GCSE 'pass' to be a grade C or above. In addition, 16 of the students said they had dropped some subjects either with or without their teachers' or their parents' consent to maximise their chances of gaining grade C or above in their other subjects.

Students were asked to talk about their courses both at school and at college. In their answers they made reference to their own attitudes and motivation, both positive and negative. This is one of the major issues discussed in detail later, but the balance of their responses was marginally on the negative side regarding their motivation at school and clearly on the positive side regarding their motivation at college. The general picture is of students who, whilst they may question their commitment at school, were ready to make the best of their current courses. On the whole, they were not disaffected though many were disappointed with progress so far.

Students offered so many comments regarding the process of transition that an illustrative survey of some of the main issues commends itself rather than a simple quantitative analysis. Institutions and individuals students make a major investment in 16+ decision making (FEFC, 1994). However, the high proportion of student choices which are frustrated raises questions about the types of career choices required by the system at this stage. This will be examined further in the section on transition and progression.

MOTIVATION

A central issue is whether these students are well set for the start of their college courses. What are they carrying with them in terms of motivation, a positive sense of their own abilities and a sense of direction in their lives? A review of motivation theory is beyond the scope of this chapter but a useful frame for the first part of this analysis of the interviews comes from the work of Covington (1992) and others who have researched the effects of motivation on learning. Covington proposes that what drives students is the social value placed on achievement or lack of achievement. His 'self-worth theory' assumes that the dominating drive is for self- acceptance and that in schools this is most often equated with the ability to achieve competitively[2]: 'In our society there is a pervasive tendency to equate accomplishment with human value, or put simply, individuals are thought to be only as worthy as their achievements' (Covington, 1992:74).

Harter (1993), in a study of low self-esteem in adolescents, describes investigations in which low self-esteem is seen to be a consequence of perceived poor performance in areas of high importance to the individual. She identifies five such areas significant for adolescent Americans: scholastic competence, athletic competence, social acceptance, behavioural conduct and physical appearance. Covington focuses on the first of these. He proposes that the high value placed on academic competence leads to a range of behaviours aimed at preserving self-worth, especially when faced with potential failure. For example, students deliberately do not make an effort or publicly claim that no effort has been expended so that failure is ascribed to lack of effort and not lack of ability. Others will set low goals so that success is almost assured, others become over strivers, so fearful of failure that they do not believe their considerable success in the past is any real indicator of ability and can only be sustained with extraordinary effort.

The categories used to describe 'self worth' preserving behaviours are based on two strands of motivation theory. Covington describes Atkinson's (1957) need achievement theory in which achievement behaviour is seen as the outcome of two 'learned drives, a motive to approach success and a motive to avoid failure' (p.28). Students differ in the balance of these drives. Those dominated by the motive to approach success will hope for, and anticipate, success and will pursue it even though they risk failure. Those dominated by the desire to avoid failure will tend to avoid the shame of failure by not pursuing achievements at all or only doing so because of external pressure such as the need to earn money.

For the second strand he uses Heider's (1958) attribution matrix, (Figure 5.1) later developed by Weiner (1970) in which the causes people offer to explain success or failure are classified. Thus a pupil may ascribe failure to lack of effort (internal, unstable). Another student might ascribe the same level of performance to lack of ability (internal, stable). The dimension of controllability/uncontrollability helps to distinguish between causes which might be classified identically against the first two: illness and lack of effort are both internal factors, but the first is uncontrollable and the second controllable.

	Locus of Causality	
Stability	Internal	External
Stable	Ability	Task ease or difficulty
Unstable	Effort	Luck

Figure 5.1 Attribution matrix (From Covington, 1992:53)

So, Covington argues, students prefer to attribute causes to their successes or failures which help them to maintain their sense of self-worth. Above all, it is preferable to attribute failure to unstable, internal or external factors than it is to attribute it to stable factors especially that of lack of ability. Students prefer to attribute failure to lack of effort, for example, rather than lack of ability. More than that, failure-avoiding students in particular will actually reduce effort to have a ready-made excuse. This gives us a frame for examining the responses of the students interviewed. What, for them, counts as success and failure, and to what do they ascribe their successes and failures?

The significance of this analysis for this study is not that any of the interviewees displayed low self-esteem but rather that, in maintaining self-esteem, they may engage in behaviour which either directly or indirectly limits achievement.

The grade C cliff

What counts as success and failure for these students? Here the answer is unequivocal. Every interviewee talked about passing and failing GCSE courses. A 'pass' was C and above and a 'fail' was below C. This understanding is so all pervasive that it was necessary to pretend to be obtuse in order to have the interviewees spell out their understanding:

Student 1	I need four GCSEs. At the moment I've got two GCSEs, Science GCSEs…
Interviewer	When you say you've got them…
Student 1	I passed them.
Interviewer	At what grade are you talking about?
Student 1	…at grade C. You need C grade and above. At the moment I've got two GCSE, C grades, and I need four to do A-Levels. So if I pass this I can get another four…

This student, who had only 'got' two GCSEs, had actually achieved grade D in five other subjects. The interviews were all punctuated with similar references: 'I had to have English and maths…', 'I was going to do A-levels, hoping to pass my GCSEs because I had a head for work', 'In French I knew I wasn't going to pass because I didn't really like French', 'You don't need any GCSEs to get on the course because it's like a GCSE anyway'. Just occasionally some of the students remembered that they had been told that any grade should be regarded as a pass but they were not convinced:

Interviewer	I am getting the impression that in some ways it was a bit of a shock when you got your results.

Student 2	Yes
Interviewer	How do you feel about it now?
Student 2	Now?...Some of the teachers in the college say E is a pass...but I failed it.
Interviewer	At the time you felt that you had failed but now you are beginning to feel better about it?
Student 2	Yes...But these grades (an A in Bengali, three Es , two Fs and a G) won't do for me to get a job.

Their attitudes to their own results varied. A few expressed satisfaction even though they did not 'pass'. Usually, this was because they managed better grades than expected. Some had 'passed' unexpectedly and were very pleased. The vast majority considered that they had failed their exams and some were embarrassed at even mentioning their grades – an E was poor, an F shaming, below F not to be mentioned:

Interviewer	(To student who has two grade Cs) What were your other results, if I may ask?
Student 3	Mostly I got all Ds. In maths I got a D. In English I got two Ds. I got D in business studies and a D in CDT and I got E in German.
Interviewer	And how did you feel about those results?
Student 3	Very disappointed. In my mocks I got fairly good results. I got Cs in my mocks, so I didn't do very well in the final exams.
Interviewer	And you were disappointed?
Student 3	Oh yes terribly disappointed. In German for example, I got B in my mocks and I came out with an E in the final exam.
Interviewer	And this was a complete surprise to you?
Student 3	Yes, a complete surprise. Because my teacher knew I'd pass with ease, but I just didn't do well in the final exam and I came out with an E.

Many spoke about the pressure they had been under at school to achieve a grade C. They were given extra coaching and mounds of revision. Some recognised the pressure on their teachers and were sympathetic. Others felt that it had been counter-productive in that they eventually gave up under the pressure of work:

Interviewer	In general did you think they (school teachers) expected too much or too little of you?
Student 4	I think it was just right.
Student 5	They expected everything to be perfect and like, because you were competing with other schools in England and if other schools were doing better than you, then it was our fault. We had to measure up to them.
Interviewer	And you didn't feel that was helpful.
Student 5	No not really. It was just more pressure for us to do better than everyone else and it just weren't happening and they knew that.
Student 6	Ds and Es aren't bad at all. You're just expected to think that Cs and Bs and As are all that counts.

For many of these students GCSE does not represent a summing up of one stage of their education but rather a barrier to be surmounted, a cliff to be climbed. The rhetoric says that GCSE is an examination for all. In fact, in terms of the meaning given to the examination, it is only those who have achieved grade C and above who are valued and it is only those subjects in which grade C or above has been achieved that a student is 'good' at. This meaning is reinforced by the system which uses grade C and above as a selection mechanism. If you climb the grade C cliff then a whole new landscape opens up. You can choose to do A-levels or advanced GNVQ or you can choose, as some did, to do intermediate GNVQ and consolidate your position.

Less than grade C and you are still at the bottom of the cliff and must start to climb again. Here there were differences between the students in the FE colleges and those in the sixth form colleges. The sixth form students, in general, had a re-sit mentality. That is, they saw themselves attempting to scale the cliff again using a combination of GNVQ and re-sit GCSE but this time with confidence and enthusiasm dented by the results they had already got: 'They said you couldn't go on to anything like A-levels but you could do re-sits. So I thought, well its better than nothing'(student 7). Their focus was A-level. The FE students, on the other hand, had a by-pass mentality. They were much more likely to have a particular vocational focus. Some had specifically rejected the A-level route, though not necessarily the ambition to go on to higher education. For these, taking GNVQ was a route round the cliff or at least a staged pathway up it. They talked about the 'modular' structure of GNVQ with its course work and end of module tests as suiting their way of working and, in some cases, they contrasted this directly with their dislike of, and inability to cope with, end of course examinations: 'And I like the course better, because with exams, if you fail your exams, you've wasted a whole year' (student 8). Students on vocational courses, however, were less concerned about their GCSE grades than they were about access to their chosen course: 'I'd wanted to be a hairdresser since I was about 8. My Aunty was a hairdresser' (student 9).

The overall impression, however, is of many students starting their post-16 education or training with a strong sense, not of building on their school achievements, but of having to start again to achieve what they should have achieved at 16.

Explaining success and failure

Because there is such a clear-cut distinction in the minds of the students between success and failure, it is possible to use the attribution matrix described above to classify the explanations given by the students for their achievements.

(a) Ability

None of the students ascribed their GCSE results to a general lack of ability. Some did admit to more specific difficulties. Several commented on their lack of ability in mathematics but even here references could be oblique: 'I never got into maths', 'maths I definitely knew I wouldn't get'. Two referred to the fact that they were entered for a limited grade examination in mathematics and that to get a grade C, 'You would have to get 100% and nobody gets that'. The oblique admission of lack of ability was used by several as an excuse for not trying in the subject: 'you cannot get a C it is not worth putting the effort in'. A number admitted to problems with spelling: 'The problem was, I'm sure my answers were right but I've got spelling problems'. So, lack of ability in a specific area can be used as an excuse for failure elsewhere. Other oblique references to ability included comments about subjects which were not liked: 'When you are not interested in something, you can't get into the work can you?...No matter how hard I worked in history I couldn't get into it', 'My French I knew for a fact that I wasn't going to pass French because I didn't, I don't really like French'.

(b) Effort

References to effort appeared in all the interviews. Students referred to the pressure put on by teachers and to their own effort or lack of effort in relation to their examination work. One student had raised his lack of effort into a lifestyle: 'It's just like I'm dead laid back'. For most, however, their effort or lack of it was used directly to explain their results: 'I think I just got out what I put in. I didn't revise and I only got three', 'My D and two Es were in maths and science, because they were my worst subjects and I never bothered with them', 'I did good in the ones I wanted to and the ones I just couldn't be bothered with I didn't bother with'. Conversely, success in gaining grades C and above would often be ascribed to positive effort. The following extract is from an interview with a student who had been told that she didn't need any C grades for the course she wanted to follow at college.

Student 10	No, I was still trying hard as I was before. As if…I was thinking about as if…I was pretending I needed to get the grades just so that I wouldn't slack off or anything.
Interviewer	It was a personal thing.
Student 10	Yes.
Interviewer	And were you pleased with the grades that you got?
Student 10	Yes. I did better than I thought I would.

And from student 11, 'If I hadn't tried hard with my RE and my English I wouldn't have got my Cs if you know what I mean'.

A number of students referred to failing in spite of making an effort: 'Drama, I put a lot of work into it and I thought I'd get a good grade but I didn't get a good grade in that anyway', 'Maths…even though I couldn't get my head round it at all and got a rubbish mark I still tried because my teacher was all right'. Eleven students referred directly to 'failing' mathematics even though they had worked hard.

(c) Task difficulty

Perhaps because of the nature of the interviews it is not easy to distinguish comments about task difficulty from comments about ability or effort. There were, however, a number of references to the problems of maintaining a range of subjects: 'There was too much to do actually. You know, 10 subjects. So much you know. And I didn't know which ones to do and which ones not to do'. Subjects would be dropped because students wanted to concentrate on those in which they were most likely to get a grade C or above (16 responses). There were a number of references to the amount of work being piled on at the end of the GCSE courses being counter-productive: 'Well at the end it got to a point were everyone had worked so hard they just couldn't work any more'.

(d) Luck

Here, the students ascribed their lack of success to a wide range of external factors. These included family circumstances, not liking the teachers, the teacher not liking them, bullying, disruption in class and changes of school. For example, three students ascribed lack of success in mathematics to changes of teacher, and two to revising the wrong things for the examination.

Effects on achievement

It is not possible to argue unequivocally that the commentaries which the students made on their results were all motivated by a desire to represent themselves in such a way that they maintained a sense of self-worth. A distinction would have to be made between attributions on the one hand, with the implication that the students consciously or unconsciously are making choices about how to present their achievements; and, on the other hand, actual events beyond the control of the students which were bound to have a negative effect. For example, a girl taken to London by her family in the term before her GCSE examinations and who was, therefore, not entered could hardly be seen as giving a 'self-worth' explanation for her lack of achievement. Similarly, changes of school and frequent changes of teacher could be statements of historical fact rather than selected attributions.

However, we believe that there is enough evidence to claim that students do feel a need to defend their self-esteem against the perceived failure at GCSE. This is not just a process of *post-hoc* explanation. Ability is clearly aligned to the achievement of grade C. Their need to preserve self-worth can be seen affecting their behaviour in the lead-up to examinations as they try to maximise their chances of high status grade Cs or to provide 'self-worth' preserving explanations for their lack of achievement. The pressure to gain grade C leads, in a significant number of cases, not to greater effort but to a reduced effort, as with those students who said that certain subjects had been dropped or had been discounted, sometimes quite early on. The focus on grade C as a pass meant that they attempted to maximise their chances, as they saw it, by concentrating on the subjects that they were good at: 'Some of the subjects like French or science, because I was getting low marks, I didn't really concentrate on them. I concentrated on the ones I thought I'd get higher marks for' (student 12).

One consequence is that the notion of a broad, balanced education really applies only to those who feel they are going to achieve grade C and above in a wide range of subjects, i.e. the brightest students. The further down the ability range the narrower the range of subjects is likely to be. The justification for 'dropping' subjects was sometimes directly expressed in vocational terms, so history and geography and sometimes languages were seen as useless: 'The qualifications that I took at school, well, I didn't think I'd ever use geography and stuff like that and biology' (student 13).

There is enough in this study for questions to be raised about the grade C bench-mark. Is it a mark of raised achievement or is it a cause of underachievement for many students, at least in some subjects?

TRANSITION AND PROGRESSION

Young (1993b) draws lessons from post-16 developments in Sweden and Finland, observing that all European and other industrialised countries are experiencing similar pressures. A recent Swedish government report on their reforms identifies a major issue on which they are based: 'there was research showing that many more pupils stayed on and fulfilled their upper secondary (post-16) education if they were allowed to go on the particular line of study which they most preferred' (Hjorth, 1995). We might reasonably argue that it is unlikely that there are basic differences in human nature between young people in Sweden and in this country; the extent to which the process of transition leaves students following a preferred line of study is a good indicator of the effectiveness of that process.

Of the students interviewed some did indicate that they were following their preferred line of study. Most of these were following specific vocational courses though some had chosen, for example,

GNVQ business studies because they wanted a general introduction to the world of business. The majority had ended up on their courses more by accident than design. In a study of transition from schooling into training it has been observed that 'choices' made by young people were more accurately described as a 'great training lottery' rather than rational decision making (Hollands, 1991). Evidence from our own interviews supports this.

Two key features recur in the responses: a desire for transparency of the process by which their achievements are measured and a desire for progression, not just for those with four or five GCSE results at grade C and above but for all students. We found four categories of responses to course choices. We should emphasise here that the students interviewed do not represent a sample of all students or even of all students with qualifications less than five grade C GCSEs. Consequently, although there is enough evidence to raise concerns, no claims are made about the relative proportions of students falling into the various categories.

First choice course

Students in this category were following a course of their choice, sometimes one which they had set their sights on some time ago:

> *Student 14* I wrote to the BBC and ITV to ask them what qualifications I'd need...I started writing to them when I was about twelve...I went on open days and then I phoned up X College and asked if I could go around again. Then I had interviews. And then I had another look round and I preferred this one.

Some students gave the impression of having arrived at a destination and that school, although necessary, was less satisfactory because they had had to do things they had not chosen: 'I didn't like school at all. I like college because I've chose to do this and so it's something I've wanted to do and so I'm enjoying it more' (student 15). This group of students illustrate an important point in relation to a culture of lifetime learning. Students with a clear focus and who achieve entry requirements for their chosen courses are much more likely to be able to exercise choice of course and college. Paradoxically, the narrower their focus, the freer they are to choose the college and the level of the course because they have clear criteria for making a choice. But the short-term advantage of a clear vocational focus may conceal a long-term disadvantage. Their narrow focus, in a period of rapid change, will seriously narrow their ultimate career options.

Late redirection

Given the selection of students for interview, significant numbers would be suspected to fail to achieve their hoped-for grades. Although, as we have seen above, they may claim that their results were more or less what they expected, in fact many were in the position of having to rethink their post-16 options after their results had come through. This includes many who fall into the other categories as well. Sometimes this led to considerable changes of direction:

> *Student 16*   I wanted to do electronics, but I didn't get three GCSEs in the exams, so they advised me that this course (GNVQ Leisure and Tourism) would be better... and go on to it (electronics) later. But I've changed my mind; I want to go on to Advanced level leisure and tourism.

Although it would appear that this redirection has worked out for this student it was by no means always the case:

> *Student 17*   I was planning to do A-levels. But my exam results let me down. So I didn't think about doing leisure and tourism. They just said, 'You can do this and it's the equivalent of four GCSEs.' I hadn't really thought about it beforehand. And if you said, 'Oh I was thinking of doing that,' they said, 'Oh this is better than that. This leisure and tourism's a lot better than that. You should do this.'

Unconvinced choice

In this category are students who have been deflected from their main focus but have not lost it completely. Typically, they would be frustrated A-level students who had not got the grades they needed and who had been redirected into GNVQ courses. These they treated instrumentally as means to re-enter the A-level programme rather than as intrinsically valuable in furthering their careers:

Student 18   I really wanted to do my A-level in biology, chemistry and RE, but because I got two Ds I couldn't. I had to choose this course and then after I might be going on to A-levels next year....And I couldn't talk to anybody about this GNVQ subject because nobody was doing it.

Confused course entry

Some students were following courses but without any sense of having found a focus or a direction. This group includes those students who would have been without focus even if they had gained grade Cs as well as those who still seem to be at the dreaming stage as far as career choice is concerned:

Student 19   I didn't do as well as I expected to in my exams, so I had to change my course. But I didn't know what I wanted to do anyway, and I still don't know what I want to do now.

Student 20   That's why I had an interview with the careers officer – because I've changed my mind about becoming a courier. I want to go into journalism....He weren't really that helpful. Aren't they meant to encourage you? He was saying, 'No' – to everything I said.

THE ROADS NOT TAKEN

Robert Frost, in his poem, 'The Road not Taken', describes a moment of decision to take the less well trodden of two paths. His decision is made with no sure knowledge of where either path leads and with an understanding that, although in theory it would be possible to return to follow the road not taken, it is unlikely that he will ever do so. It is only in theory that decision making can be made to fit a rational model (Weick, 1979). As for practice, adults are more likely to recognise some truth in Crozier and Friedberg's generalisations, broad though they be: 'Men, decision makers in particular, never know very clearly what they want....They discover their aims, which are frequently new to them, through experience, i.e. by making decisions' (Crozier and Friedberg, 1980).

We should perhaps beware of proposing that the system should be so tight that students cannot be surprised into discovering what it is they want to make of their lives. On the other hand, there is something odd about a system which invests so much in the processes of transfer, careers officers, information from colleges, careers lessons, visits and interviews and yet leaves many students drifting because of surprises in their examination results. One piece of research among Year 11 pupils found that the vast majority across the ability range took for granted the value of continuing in full-time education (Taylor, 1992). The numbers actually staying on would bear this out. And yet GCSE is still treated for selection purposes as if it is O-level, a system set up to mark progress towards matriculation and consequently university entrance. Its value, its meaning for the students, is almost entirely tied to this notion. A consequence is that most students feel they have failed in whole or in part. It should be remembered that even those students with five grade Cs were probably entered for nine or 10 GCSE examinations and will consider themselves to have failed some subjects. One might even suggest that those students who do not have any hope of grade Cs are better off in transition terms in that they at least can plan their futures without waiting for that fateful day in August to see whether they will be allowed to pursue their preferred programme.

MATTERS ARISING

Chaos or coherence

The 1980s and early 1990s were a period of innovation or, more precisely, innovations. Few people would deny that there was a need to change. Many would also argue that a multi-agency approach was also needed to avoid the traps of central planning and the consequent dangers of over-prescription and lack of flexibility. Centralised control of innovations has been based on industrial entrepreneurial models, forcing change by setting targets and tying funding to the achievement of those goals. The problem is that such an approach, whilst promoting much interesting practice, has left us with systems, schools, colleges, examination boards and so on, at best working to their own ends and at worst with a vested interest in preserving a confusing diversity.

At the level of systems, innovation is not hazard free. Gleeson (1980) and Hyland (1991) warn against the dangers of seeing schools and colleges in mechanistic terms during periods of rapid expansion. Well-intentioned moves at reform without attention to the interrelationships of contexts leads to innovation without change (Hodkinson, 1991). Without an overall post-16 curriculum strategy at national level, national agencies and individual institutions developing their own 'frameworks for coherence' may contribute new forms of incoherence (Young, 1994). They might also imply coherence where none exists.

An illustration of this false coherence appeared in the *Guardian* of March 23 1995. To coincide with Human Resource Development Week, the paper published its guide to the 'Wheel of Qualifications'[3]. At the centre of the wheel is the foundation level where NVQ1, Foundation GNVQ and four GCSEs grades D to G are considered equivalent. Presumably for the purpose of neatness the designers of the wheel chose to ignore both the great range of attainment represented by the D to G grades and also the large numbers of pupils who fall in the gap between the first level and the second level which they give as five GCSEs at grades A to C, a gap which includes virtually all those students entering GNVQ advanced courses and many on the intermediate courses as well (FEU, 1994).

This papering over of cracks is indicative of the problem. There is a tension between the need to make continuing education and training seem coherent and progressive, and the vested interests in diversity which the entrepreneurial approach encourages. This tension is itself only one of many dilemmas facing the education and training system. Transition is a major issue, not because large numbers of young people have suddenly seen the academic light but because they have nowhere else to go. As Shaw and Bloomer (1993:82) put it:

...the system can no longer 'cool out' the less academically able or committed into employment, with their largely cheerful acceptance.... The system is outgrowing its cultural assumptions, despite the fact that these are deeply embedded in institutional arrangements and pedagogical practices.

In a comparative analysis of education in Britain, France and Japan, Green (1993:45) found that educational achievement could not be ascribed to simple causes but rather to a host of interrelating factors in the education system itself and in its social context:

It is the interaction of these factors, rather than any particular practices in education, which would seem to determine the levels of achievement characteristic of different systems.

If these interviews are typical, then one of the reasons for the initial success of GNVQ is that it has presented at least the appearance of coherence. Whether it is used as an alternative route to A-level or to university, or whether it is seen as a route through to employment, it does at least offer comprehensible and promised routes. The key to its success will be whether those promises are kept given the complex, confusing and unpredictable context in which they must operate.

Progression in learning

Grade requirements in 16+ examinations condemn students to face a stiff and uncertain obstacle course at a stage in life when supportive continuity in learning would be more appropriate. Given the aim of encouraging young people to embrace lifetime learning, it seems counter-productive to condemn a majority as failures, and to do this at a stage in their lives when there are no options other than further learning. Within the system, there are some small-scale developments (e.g. value added methods in assessment and guidance) aimed at supporting learning at 16+ (Spours and Young, 1994). There is research evidence that the optimism of youth prevails despite the toils pre-16 of 8–10 separate subject examination courses. Among students completing questionnaires during induction into a tertiary college, before direct experience of the college courses they had chosen, the greater proportion anticipated and preferred interactive learning activities (Bloomer and Morgan, 1993). Those authors, however, fear that too much curriculum planning and implementation is based on mechanistic input/output models; students may find the rhetoric at variance with their in-course experience.

FE students in both academic and vocational groups are sensitive to curricular provision. Avis (1991a) argues that there is a need for academic practice to recover its critical potential by overcoming its separation from the social world, and to guard against the perception of knowledge as a disposable commodity rather than a means of interpreting and engaging in the social world. The students we interviewed frequently articulated an instrumental approach to learning which they perceived as a requirement for short-term progression within the system. This is a long way from identifying themselves with lifetime learning.

Take, as an example, the way in which subjects, pre-16, are dismissed by many students as not being of any use. History and geography come high on this list. Travel and tourism and business studies students both dismissed the humanities as being of no value despite the obvious links to both occupational areas. This is tied, as we argued above, to the need to maximise the number of grade Cs. The dismissal of some subjects as useless can be seen as a rationalisation of that process. The interviewees had difficulty in seeing school learning as intrinsically valuable. In spite of the explicit recognition of the majority that they had learnt a great deal at school, their assessment of the value of their schooling had, for many, become entirely caught up in the instrumental value of examination grades.

Learning contracts

The introduction of the word 'contract' to the discussion is a recognition of the interdependence of learners and teachers in the context of a common culture, not another business approach to education. As part of their admissions processes, some colleges require applicants to sign individual student contracts detailing the course, which has been negotiated, and summarising the responsibilities of both the college staff and the individual student. These are not commercial contracts and indeed they are renegotiable at any stage but they do represent a new type of relationship between students and college staff, one in which both have rights and responsibilities.

These new types of working relationships might be seen as one aspect of the emerging culture of lifetime learning. Of their nature, educational processes are not forced but flourish within relationships in which interdependence is at least implicitly recognised. The adoption of the term culture in a democratic society as a metaphor for change in education and training points away from attempts to restrict and direct the lives of others towards co-operation and understanding and towards a recognition that we operate in multiple social contexts. One aspect of this mutual understanding must be a recognition of the needs of individuals to retain a sense of self-worth and to be provided with the circumstances in which their achievements, at whatever level, are valued and built on. The college/ individual student contracts are a brave rhetoric in the face of confusion at national level. The evidence of this study is that, for many students, there is no sense of a 'contract' between students and providers within the education and training system.

CONCLUDING COMMENTS

Purely on the evidence of this small-scale research, it would be presumptuous to make any recommendation other than the need to continue to gather evidence from the students themselves. However, much work has already been done and we end with our own contribution to what Gleeson (Chapter 2) calls a 'third educational settlement.'

(a) Take student goals seriously

There is a growing body of research which builds on the skills of goal setting (Edwards, 1989; Fazey, 1993; Pintrich and De Groot, 1990; Schunk and Gaa, 1981; Zimmerman, 1989). Examples in practice include 14–19 and higher education. Developments in negotiated academic guidance have been supported by TVEI and recording achievement where it has had a strong staff development base. In higher education a student-driven model of learning contracts with providers of sandwich placements has been developed to earn academic credit towards degrees (Marshall, 1991) and negotiating learning goals has been central to a contracted grades experiment in teacher education in a Canadian College (Hallinan and Danaher, 1994). On the other hand Hodkinson and Sparkes (1995a) in their evaluation of Youth Credits show how formalised 'technical rational' models of decision making are at odds with the 'pragmatic rational' means by which young people actually make decisions. Taking goal setting seriously means understanding how young people make decisions. Goal setting must take account of cultural and economic contexts.

(b) Be honest about what is on offer

The provision of A-levels and Advanced level GNVQ is currently supported by a false rhetoric of 'parity of esteem'. It undermines notions of justice and agreed learning goals in a manner which is rightly described as not merely ambiguous but less than honest (Young, 1994). For all the high aspirations of the post-16 framework proposed by Sir Ron Dearing in his interim report (Dearing, 1995), parity of esteem cannot be given by government edict. It will have to be earned. What students want to know is that they can make progress, that they are following a programme which does not lead up a blind alley.

(c) Make the means of making progress as transparent as possible

Opting for modular courses and course work is one way, we would suggest, that students make a reasonable request for transparency. They wish to know how their work is valuable and is to be valued. This, unfortunately, is in contrast with the return to end-on examinations and the reduction in the value of course work at GCSE level, with the consequent effect of obscuring from students the means by which their grades are achieved. As many will say, the great lost opportunity of the review of post-16 qualifications is the fact that it is just post-16. The problems of drop-out and low aspirations which Dearing's interim report on education and training addresses do not begin at 16, nor will any effective action to overcome those problems.

Any 'contract' must be subject to a number of caveats related to unknowns such as future employment prospects and the availability of places in higher education and this should be made plain. But what should also be plain is the way that a commitment to learning, for all students whatever their starting point, achieves both the intrinsic satisfaction of becoming more knowledgeable and more able and the instrumental purpose of accumulating credit towards qualifications and employment.

NOTES

1. This is an interpretation of the information in the FEU report (1994) and is based on the assumption that, given the actual qualifications of students on GNVQ intermediate and advanced courses, it is most likely that they would have been directed towards GCSE re-sits or courses such as BTEC first and national courses in the absence of GNVQ.
2. It should be remembered here that Covington is taking his examples from the American system which is based more on regular competitive grading than the system in England and Wales.
3. The *Guardian's* sources were the Institute of Personnel and Development and the Business and Technology Education Council. The wheel itself is impressive, purporting to show the coherence between the levels of qualifications along three routes – academic, occupational and vocational. Occupational qualifications, we are told, are National Vocational Qualifications. Vocational qualifications on the other hand are General National Vocational

Qualifications which are defined in the 1994 White Paper as 'preparing young people for employment in broad occupational areas'.

Core Skills – The Continuing Debate

Rob Halsall

INTRODUCTION

The core skills initiative clearly stems from government and industry concern as to the suitability of curricula and qualifications for employment and the economy (e.g. CBI, 1989; DES, 1989). This was a concern shared by many practitioners who recognised that vocational awards focused too narrowly on skills specific to a particular vocational context and that the A-level experience was too specialised. In one sense, then, core skills were seen by some as a means of addressing the issue of breadth by their incorporation into existing curricula and qualifications. This approach won the day over an alternative radical reform of these. It is also possible to interpret the initiative as constituting an attempt to bridge the academic and vocational divide. As Coates (1991:45) points out in relation to the CBI report, the issues of core skills and transference between academic and vocational routes were linked:

> If core skills were to be a common feature of all courses and qualifications...it seemed that they would increase the compatibility of academic and vocational qualifications, and might provide a basis for transfer....This second purpose of core skills was to be given increased emphasis as the initiative developed.

Underpinning these two purposes are the governments' aims to increase the number of young people in further education and training, to include a vocational component in their course and to produce a more 'employable' workforce. However, as indicated in Chapter 2 the government's policy on 14–19 education contains inconsistencies and tensions, not least because of clashes of interest and ideology. At the broadest level there is the fact that, 'Government rhetoric on meeting the country's needs implies sweeping curricular change...defence of the traditional A level system suggests that only vocational courses need to be reformed' (Macfarlane, 1993: xiv-xv). In this context it is hardly surprising to find inconsistencies and tensions surrounding specific initiatives within the overall reforms. The development of core skills is a good case in point. It is also an important case given its direct relevance to the government aims outlined above, and to its purported role in responding to the emerging post-Fordist economy where flexibility, adaptability, transferability, communication skills and teamwork are viewed as essential traits. The following two sections outline the development of the core skills initiative. Therafter, this chapter seeks to explore a number of issues concerning the initiative.

DEVELOPMENT OF THE CORE SKILLS INITIATIVE

There is nothing new in recommendations for some sort of core skills element in education and training but current thinking can be traced back to the late 1970s and early 1980s. Of particular influence in that period was *A Basis For Choice* (FEU, 1979) which recommended a core entitlement of knowledge and skills, and various MSC-funded projects including its Core Skills Project begun in 1984. Thus, a position was reached where, '...a core of related knowledge, skills, qualities and attitudes has featured in the requirements of BTEC, the TVEI and the CPVE' (Maclure, 1991: 38).

A flurry of activity in 1989 served to sharpen the debate. In February of that year, the then Secretary of State, Kenneth Baker, delivered his 'New Strategy' speech (DES, 1989) in which he argued for a broad education post-16 and for a central role in this of a set of core skills comprising communication, numeracy, personal relations (oriented especially to teamwork and leadership), familiarity with technology, familiarity with systems (principally those of the workplace) and familiarity with changing working and social contexts. He also proposed that these skills should be integrated into learning programmes, that they should be assessed and that assessment should form the basis of a credit transfer system between academic and vocational awards. All three proposals have since been pursued consistently. This speech was soon followed by two key publications which also argued for core skills implementation. The HMI paper on post-16 core skills (DES, 1989) suggested that they be: knowledge about information technology (IT), using IT, knowledge about society and the environment, knowledge about industry and commerce, numeracy, communication, problem-solving, practical skills, working co-operatively and adaptability. The CBI, in the light of its views regarding narrowly based education and training qualifications (especially A-levels and National Vocational Qualifications (NVQs)), its regret at the non-implementation of the Higginson Report and its worries that the National Curriculum might neglect cross-curricular themes, produced a similar list of core skills to HMI, adding positive attitudes to change and values and integrity (CBI, 1989).

Finally, in 1989, there came a request to the National Curriculum Council (NCC) and the School Examinations and Assessment Council (SEAC) from Baker's successor, John MacGregor, for promotion of the inclusion of core skills into post-16 provision. The NCC subsequently produced a recommendation for six core skills: communication, numeracy, IT, problem-solving, personal skills and modern language competence (NCC, 1990). This was endorsed by the SEAC and by the National Council for Vocational Qualifications (NCVQ) which had become increasingly sensitive to criticisms concerning the narrowness of its NVQs.

It is apparent from the above that the core skills initiative can be seen as having contributed to the bringing together of different bodies responsible for education and training. However, as Macfarlane points out, 'The apparent consensus over the common ground does …conceal significant differences in the extent to which academic and vocational courses are receptive to the concept of transferable core skills' (1993:56).

There are some interesting core skills developments within the A-level context as demonstrated, for example, in the CROSSMAPS programme assessment mapping system which is being used both to identify achievements across A-level programmes in 10 core skills areas and to identify suitable enrichment courses and activities which can provide opportunities to achieve those core skill elements not being delivered through the chosen A-levels (for example, Morgan, 1993). However, the incorporation of core skills into A-levels is distinctly patchy and the most comprehensive attempt at applying them is clearly within GNVQ programmes.

GNVQ CORE SKILLS

GNVQ core skills are defined as:

> …personal transferable skills which play an important part in developing

the effective performance of the individual in a wide range of vocational contexts. They offer the potential for enhancing transfer of learning by making learners more aware of the skills they possess and of the skills which are required in different contexts. Core skills are those generic skills which are used in carrying out all tasks and activities, whether in education and training, at work or in life in general. (BTEC, 1993a:57)

There are six core skills units, each available at five levels and each comprising elements of achievement which specify the detailed skills, knowledge and understanding which underpin performance. Each element has a number of performance criteria defining successful performance; range statements which place limits around the areas of knowledge/performance in which achievements are expected and which refer to the contexts in which learners need to show achievement; and evidence indicators which suggest suitable forms of evidence and indicate requirement for sufficiency. The core skills units have variable status. To achieve a GNVQ at any level the minimum requirement is the achievement of the three core skills units designated as mandatory at the level of the GNVQ, e.g. level 3 unit for a GNVQ 3 (Advanced Vocational), though candidates can achieve beyond that level. The mandatory core skills units are Communication, Information Technology and Application of Number. Centres are also encouraged to develop and assess Personal Skills – Working with Others, Personal Skills – Improving Own Learning and Performance and Problem Solving. Detailed specifications of each unit have been available since July 1993 (e.g. BTEC, 1993b).

Although the six sets of elements are presented and described as core skills units:

> Wherever possible core skills should be delivered in an integrated way... should permeate the learning and assessment activities which make up the GNVQ programme. Vocational activities should be designed to create opportunities for learners to generate and collect evidence which provides comprehensive coverage of core skills. (BTEC, 1993a:60)

In short, it is recommended that specifications are mapped against GNVQ vocational units to ensure coverage of the core skills units. Where aspects of core skills cannot be achieved through projects, assignments and other activities designed for vocational units, other learning opportunities can be identified.

ISSUES SURROUNDING CORE SKILLS

Consistency, transferability and comparability

If we return to the definition of GNVQ core skills given in the previous section it is clear that the terms core, transferable and generic skills are being used interchangeably and that these skills are seen as contributing to transfer of learning and effective performance in different contexts. A number of key questions can be posed. *Are* core, transferable and generic skills – and, indeed, cross-curricular – one and the same? *Do* they contribute to learning transfer and are they comparable between different contexts? Are the GNVQ core skills consistent with one another, or are they different things? What about *transferring* skills? For present purposes it will be assumed here that the terms are interchangeable though this is a rich field for debate by philosophers of education. Here, the focus is on the issues of consistency, transfer and comparability.

Are core skills those which can be applied across different subjects or across different educational, occupational and social contexts, or both? It seems difficult to consider all of the GNVQ core skills in the same way in answering this question. Thus fewer aspects of numeracy and IT are applicable across different subjects than is the case with the other core skills. And while communication and personal skills are used in all social situations, for example, and problem-solving in many, numeracy and IT again figure far less prominently. In short, these two skills or sets of skills seem to be of a different order from the others.

But how are core skills distinguished from one another within GNVQ programmes? It is through the identification of some as mandatory and others as optional or additional units, as described earlier. Hence, communication, numeracy and IT units *must* be achieved through a GNVQ programme to qualify for the award, while the other three units are not a requirement. Given the claims made concerning transferability in GNVQs and the differences between the core skills argued above in relation to transferability, the distinction made by the NCVQ needs to be questioned. Indeed, this point is reinforced if one considers other claims made about GNVQs. For example, if the promotion of learner autonomy is a central aim of these programmes it is arguably the case that personal skills and problem-solving should be of at least equal status to the other core skills.

There is also the issue of whether any particular core skill is applicable in exactly the same way across different subjects and situations. For example, is there a specific skill or set of skills of problem-solving? Do we solve all problems by applying a given set of problem-solving techniques or do we apply skills relevant to a particular problem? Can the health care specialist, for instance, solve an engineering problem and is either expert necessarily capable of solving domestic problems be they to do with a breakdown in the central heating system or dealing with troublesome adolescents? It is clearly the case that a key aim of core skills implementation is to provide learners with generic, transferable skills. An Employment Department Research and Development Report (DoE, 1993:9) states that, 'the core skills movement...assumes that it is possible to identify generic skills that are transferable across education and work contexts and that the acquisition of such skills will enhance learner flexibility, adaptability and autonomy'. However, there is little empirical or philosophical evidence to suggest that core skills are transferable to all contexts and learning activities; at best they have broad applicability. Resnick (1987b:118) points out that:

> Cognitive research yields repeated demonstrations that specific content and knowledge plays a central role in reasoning, thinking and learning of all kinds....General skills may be impossible to apply...if one does not have a store of knowledge about similar problems.

Philosophers of education have, generally, argued that success in one domain of knowledge will be insufficient to enable transfer to another. Thus, Barrow (1987:192) claims that, 'Since what constitutes sound critical thought or creative expression in one area...differs from what constitutes it in another...it follows that a necessary condition of being critical or creative is understanding of particular domains'. Of course, it is difficult to draw the boundaries between different domains. Any epistemological theory rests upon one of several possible classifications of knowledge. In any case, it can be argued that the relevance of core skills does not need to be based either on a supposition that they can be exercised in the absence of subject content (indeed, in most curricula they are not meant to be 'delivered' as separate units), or on a claim that they are exactly the same thing in different contexts. There are, in fact, generic processes involved in these skills. As Coates (1991:47) says, in relation to problem-solving, there is the commonality of 'being methodical or rational, being used to experimenting and thinking for oneself'.

It is likely, therefore, that there will be *some* skill transference: the development of a skill in a different context will probably be achieved more rapidly than would otherwise be the case as a result of prior experience in applying those commonalities that do exist. Thus, Bridges (1993:48) argues that:

> the claim may be simply that there is some thing in common between approaches to problem-solving...and that developing this in one area can therefore contribute to, but not be sufficient for, its development in other areas.

Nevertheless, there are implications here. Because a core skill in one context is not directly comparable with the same skill in another context, we must beware of making assumptions concerning learners' abilities in core skills as they move into different programme areas. In particular, if core skills are not fully comparable between different contexts we need to consider carefully practices relating to credit transfer and admission with advanced standing. Can the credit awarded for a core skill in one programme provide exemption from any credit points in that core skill within a different programme? Coates (1991:51) answers this question thus:

> The requirement that core skills should not be detached from their context...decides the question of whether core skills would provide credit transfer between different qualifications...if core skills are never assessed separately from occupational performance, then the problem-solving unit (in bricklaying) provides no exemption from any part of the tractor-driving assessment.

Finally in this section, assuming that to some extent at least one can apply core skills in a variety of contexts, what of the skills which enable that transfer to take place? Fleming (1991:10–11) describes these as meta-competences:

> competences which work on other competences...the person with a meta-competence has...a bird's eye view of the particular competence which allows them to recognise that it depends on a conjuncture of circumstances that can and probably will change. Even more importantly, the need for change...will be more readily seen and acted upon....It's...a critical, adaptable perspective on, and ability to manipulate, one's own competences.

Little attention has been given to this notion. Certainly, there is little in the way of any systematic approach at encouraging or testing its development. Fleming argues that we need to improve our understanding of how knowledge 'transforms itself into meta-competence and where lower order competences fit into this' (Fleming, 1991:11).

The existing notions of performance criteria and range do not appear to be helpful or adequate in developing the learner's ability to recontextualise his or her own competence or skill. Much work is needed to move forward here. A useful start has been made by Bridges (1993:50–51) who suggests that this will involve attention to, at the very least:

> 1)...the discernment of similarities and differences between one social/cognitive setting and another;
> 2)...whatever cognitive equipment it is which enables someone to modify, extend or adapt a previous repertoire...to the different requirements of the new situation;
> 3)...the attitudes or dispositions which support both of these – perhaps a combination of...receptiveness and sensitivity...confidence or enterprise.

This last point brings us back of course to the earlier discussion concerning the distinction made between different core skills, for surely it is an argument in favour of the primacy of personal skills! However, it is pertinent to point out that other writers are dismissive of the notion of meta-competence, locating their views within a wider critique of competence approaches. Thus, Barnett (1994:81) contends that, 'Even the idea of metacompetences...does not take us much further forward....For whether meta or not, competences will remain behaviours and capacities to act as desired and defined by others', while Hyland (1994:26) suggests that meta-competence is an implausible notion which is as problematic as that of core skills: 'If there is a sense in which the idea of generic competence may be described as logical nonsense, then meta-competence is a prime candidate for the label...of "nonsense on stilts"'.

The academic–vocational divide

A powerful attack on NCVQ qualifications was made by Smithers (1993) who, in turn, was criticised for his slim evidential base and for misunderstanding the nature of the programmes of study. However, many of the points he made were repeated by the FEFC (1994) and OFSTED (1994). There is little doubt that the reforms put in place by, or through, the NCVQ have been underfunded and instituted too rapidly. There have also been problems associated with the rapid increase of students opting to take GNVQs. The NCVQ has introduced a number of 'adjustments' since the FEFC and OFSTED inspections and expects these to address the issues raised. However, even if 'teething troubles' are overcome, will the academic–vocational divide be bridged? The fact of the matter is that we are left with a diverse and differentiated curriculum in the post-16 sector. This is to be replicated, in the wake of Dearing's review of the national curriculum, in the 14–16 sector.

Despite its rhetoric, the Tory government is reluctant to introduce radical changes. It is particularly reluctant to abandon the 'gold standard' of A-levels. The Secretary of State's recent remit to Sir Ron Dearing as chair of SCAA (April 1995) to review post-16 provision illustrates the government's 'angst'. It recognises the need for reform, but in signalling the need to maintain the rigour of A-levels and build on the two vocational qualification routes it appears to shy away from anything too radical that would offend opposition from within the Conservative party. Indeed, at the Secondary Heads Association conference in Warwick in the week preceding the review's announcement, the Secretary for State made it clear that the three-track qualifications system was here to stay.

Consequently, there is as yet no immediate proposal to introduce a single qualification for post-16 or 14–19 education, and as Avis (1992:365) contends, 'Whilst (recent) changes are more than merely cosmetic and hold progressive potential they, nevertheless, should be considered as adaptive and technical rather than transformative'. Hyland (1994:113) adds that, 'all the signs are that the incrementalist approach to reform represented by GNVQs will not bring about the sort of foundational changes necessary to upgrade vocational studies and bridge the vocational/academic gulf'.

One strand of that incremental reform is the use of core skills to underpin all 16–19 courses so as to encourage greater integration between different programmes and ministers have responded positively to calls for this from the National Advisory Council for Education and Training Targets, as illustrated by the White Paper, *Forging Ahead* (1995). However, the most that can be expected from this is some minor modification to A-levels. Here, it is worth noting that it is only the core skills of literacy, numeracy and information technology that are pursued in relation to the assessment of A-level candidates. Certainly, it does not seem at present that significant groups of people – including employers, HE personnel, the students themselves and their parents – are regarding NVQs and GNVQs as equivalent to their academic counterparts. Also, how substantial credit transfer between different programmes will be, following Dearing's review of 16–19 education and training (Dearing, 1995), remains to be seen.

A number of writers have argued that the only way to bridge the academic–vocational divide is to impose a common curriculum, or at least a common curriculum framework, and to develop a common award such as the General Education Diploma as recommended by the National Commission on Education (1993). Thus, from a *Times Higher Education Supplement* editorial (1994:11):

> Tinkering with 'teething problems' may well improve the current provision of GNVQs, but it is unlikely to lead to the provision of a comprehensible and comprehensive post-compulsory education and training system....What is needed is a single system which would allow a constructive coagulation of the virtues of the GNVQ...and A-level.

Hyland (1994) has suggested a common core for all at 14–16 including an education for work component; a post-16 stage in which vocational and general elements are available for specialisation but in which overlap and transfer are possible, and in which all elements are underpinned by the knowledge and breadth of learning which characterise the *baccalaureat* and *Abitur;* the introduction of the General Education Diploma and the formation of a single body with responsibility for education and training. This is similar to recommendations made by the Institute for Public Policy Research (1990) which proposed a British baccalaureat based on a modular curriculum comprising a common core of content, skills and processes, together with specialist choices. Students would take modules from each of three domains of study – social and human sciences, natural sciences and technology and arts, language and literature – and pursue at least one area in greater depth. All students would also undertake work experience or community service elements.

The proposals in Dearing's interim report on education and training are nowhere as radical as either of the above suggestions. A change of government might eventually bring about much more sweeping reform, though in his lecture at the London Institute of Education (23 July 1995), Tony Blair indicated that the Labour party is contemplating something less radical: the creation of a post-14 qualifications system that would allow students to combine academic and vocational study and that would incorporate 'compatible curriculum structures and common principles of assessment'. Would such a change be sweeping enough? Here, the question needs to be raised as to whether radical reform is the best or most appropriate way forward. Is it not possible that further 'tinkering' with existing programmes to achieve greater commonality between them, rather than some form of coalescence, is still a valuable option? Has sufficient account been taken of the views of teachers, students and parents, or would employers, the government and, indeed, many academics prefer not to search too intensely here?

There are limitations in both academic and vocational programmes which could be attended to. The existence of these does not constitute an *a priori* case for radical change. Many proponents of such change advance their proposals in the light of concerns that the academic–vocational divide is a reflection of the class system; they believe that only some version of a common curriculum can eradicate the prejudices that produce a different status for different programmes. There is a real tension here between the principles of equity and choice and there is a real danger of ignoring what students want from the system and what might benefit them most. In any case, if radical reform is not on the agenda, attention must be paid to what might constitute the most useful form of 'tinkering'.

Arguably, the most fundamental imperative is to ensure that students maximise their learning. Despite the inadequacies of the vocational curricula, including the core skills dimension, these skills, which Avis admits are more than cosmetic, are more systematically approached in the vocational curriculum than elsewhere. It is the pursuance of such skills that might enhance the potential to at least reduce the divisive treatment and differential status of our learners. As Hodkinson (1989:380–81) argues:

a focus on personal effectiveness, autonomy and co-operation offers several advantages....Firstly, it is already seen by many as a fundamental purpose of education generally...second...it is equally valid for all students...whatever courses they follow. Thus it removes at least one example of divisive, differential treatment of different groups. Thirdly, the principle is central...to both the education and training ideologies....Perhaps most important of all, it provides a unified set of principles which can be used as a touchstone to guide our procedures at all levels. That these principles happen to underpin several recent but beleaguered curriculum initiatives...needs to be articulated.

For many years now it has been argued that A-level students have had insufficient breadth of education (e.g. DES, 1988). The core skills initiative does represent a thrust which demands at least some attention to continuing work in numeracy, communication and IT, as well as focusing specifically on problem-solving, personal skills, action-planning and evaluation. The initiative is flawed in practice but it is too easy to be totally dismissive of the notion. One of the greatest pities is that some 'liberal educators' seem to be doing their utmost to maintain perceived differences between education and training rather than to recognise both the strengths or shortcomings in each. Hodkinson (1989:373) suggests that:

> This may be partly due to a desire to preserve status, through a hierarchical view of the nature of knowledge where 'thinking' rates higher than 'doing'. It may also reflect the defensiveness of many liberal educators who feel that their basic values are under attack.

Equally, of course, it has to be said that too many practitioners in the 'vocational camp' are still too reluctant to offer a critique of their own curricula; witness, for example, some head-in-the-sand reactions to Smithers (1993). 'Standing on the hill-tops' is a negative stance which surely will impede curriculum development and improvement.

Reductivism

The competence movement generally has been seen by some commentators as atomistic, deconstructing activities into allegedly constituent skills via a process of functional analysis which breaks activities down until they are usable as 'standards'. In this respect the core skills elements for GNVQs do not differ significantly from programme-specific elements. To Jones and Moore (1993:388):

> such disaggregating techniques...produce impoverished and simplistic accounts of complex social interactions. By decontextualising 'skills' and

abstracting them from their constitutive cultural practices, these reductive procedures construct partial, disembedded representations of the complex social interactions of work and elsewhere.

The result, it is argued, is a curriculum which focuses upon technical competency to the exclusion of such dimensions as consideration of the values and role of practitioners or the goals and ethos of institutions. It might be expected that such consideration would find a place within core skills if nowhere else in NCVQ programmes. However, the nearest one comes is in the communication element on reading and responding to written material and images and even here it is only at 'level five' where this 'task' is expected to be undertaken in a way which recognises 'the factors which influence own and others' interpretations'. More generally, while reflective and reviewing skills might not be ignored they are focused upon achievement of the technical competences, rather than being a means of raising questions about, for example, the wider context in which one operates or, indeed, the validity of the set of competences and the values that underlie them. Moreover, and this point lies at the heart of notions relating to learner autonomy, the competences are not only technical but almost always totally prescribed. Learners might have scope for action-planning, reviewing and selecting resources to meet learning needs, but only within the constraints provided by prescribed outcomes. Where lies autonomy if one cannot formulate one's own objectives, at least for some of the time?

These arguments need to be taken seriously. As regards the issue of technical competency there is much to be learned from a number of responses by teacher-educators to the NCVQ model. Initial teacher training (ITT) courses have much in common with competence-based vocational programmes. In particular, a large part of these courses is given over to on-the-job training and many competences are assessed by direct observation of performance. However, competences do not stand alone in the preparation of teachers. They are:

> related to a view of knowledge and professional practice. Each is grounded in a range of values which are...pluralistic or controversial...they will be used in ways that cannot be predetermined. They will be used in different educational circumstances and within a wider educational perspective than a simple use of common sense or consensual application. (The Manchester Metropolitan University, 1993a)

Fundamental to effective teaching is the development of breadth and depth of knowledge and skills; a range of professional values, relating to, for example, the promotion of equal opportunities and recognition of the need to respect the beliefs and values of others; and self-awareness, which, among other things, involves taking account of a variety of situations and circumstances in which the skills of teaching are used. The key points are that skills must not be decontextualised and that the concept of the reflective practitioner needs to be central to the development of the effective teacher. In discussing higher education learning generally, Barnett (1994:81) states that:

> What is required...is *less* competence and more critical reflection....A genuine higher education for the professions will not be content with reflecting the professionally defined competences but will insert alternative modes of reasoning, action and reflection into the curriculum.

In order to address these points a competency-based model must be developed which is more than a list of specific tasks. Some useful work has commenced with the development of ITT competence frameworks. Here, it is worth referring to the deliberations of the working group on competences as part of the review of ITT in Northern Ireland (Department of Education, Northern Ireland, 1992:4):

> We began to see that a simple list of competences...could not convey the totality of what we wanted to say about the professional competence of a teacher...the atomisation of professional knowledge, judgement and skill into discrete competences inevitably fails to capture the essence of professional competence.

Their way forward has been to identify competences relating to knowledge (e.g. of children, learning, subject, curriculum, teacher's role) and professional skills (e.g. classroom methodology, class management, assessment and recording), and to identify the underlying qualities of the teacher 'which enable him or her to pull the individual competences together and apply them.' These qualities relate to professional values, professional and personal development, communication and relationships and synthesis and application. In similar vein has been the 'alternative' competence format devised by the ASSET programme in social work at Anglia Polytechnic University. Here, the decision was to specify core assessment criteria which bring together individual competences. These comprise commitment to professional values, continuous professional learning, affective awareness, effective communication, executive effectiveness, synthesis of knowledge and intellectual flexibility. As Winter (1992:114) puts it, 'educational criteria derived from an elaborated theory of the reflective professional practitioner'. In these ways the contextualisation of skills, the issue of values, and the reflective imperative are being taken on board. It is perhaps only with the reflective imperative that the NCVQ framework has made much headway and, arguably, only here through such initiatives as the optional core skills within GNVQs.

Of course, any competence framework, and not least that of the NCVQ, is useful in that it can help focus students' reflections on their own learning and practice. It can also be important in helping both staff and students to focus more systematically on whether opportunities are, in fact, being provided to assist the development of learning. Certainly, the NCVQ framework has also been in the vanguard in terms of making explicit what we expect students to learn and about the criteria against which assessments will be made. Nor should its obsession with the performance dimension be totally derided. A liberal education includes an understanding of different forms or realms of knowledge which might be valued for their own sake and which provide a basis for critical and creative thinking. Does it, though, enable people to understand the choices they have, to make choices and to pursue these? Bridges (1993:44–45) maintains that while the characteristics of a liberal education:

> say a great deal about (understanding and making choices) they say very little about how people are going to act in and upon a social world…even for the student who has relatively successful experience of the kind of liberal education referred to, this would still not be a sufficient condition for his or her positive freedom or liberation within most real social settings….It is precisely because education should enable people to exercise positive freedom…that we need to take seriously some of the aspirations which are expressed in contemporary educational debate in terms of skills.

It is in the context of such benefits that any reductivist critique of competence approaches, including the NCVQ framework, needs to be set. Indeed it is because of them that increasing numbers of people are recognising the value of using competences in at least some aspects of their work. However, it does seem clear that there is a need to recognise the importance of less tangible knowledge, skills, understandings and attitudes than the NCVQ framework presently embraces. The GNVQ optional core skills have their limitations and are in need of review in the light of criticisms made here and elsewhere. But they do have the potential to facilitate reflective and collaborative learning and to enable people to act in and upon the social world. This does highlight some inconsistency within GNVQs which needs to be addressed. The fact of the matter is that these core skills are optional rather than mandatory (as, indeed, they are to be within A-levels, given the 1995 White Paper's reference to the assessment of A-level candidates in the mandatory core skills alone). There is a strong argument for boosting their status. Moreover, none of the core skills are formally or directly assessed, though Hayes (1994:20) has argued that, 'There is clearly a direct correlation between the (GNVQ) grading themes and the (optional) core skills'.

One way forward in terms of addressing these concerns might be to consider the removal of core skills as separate units and, instead, bring together at least some of the core skill elements, the existing grading themes of planning, information gathering/handling and evaluation skills and other qualities not yet captured within GNVQs into a set of overarching assessment criteria applicable to all units. The result would be to bring the GNVQ model more in line with that described earlier in relation to the ASSET programme and some of the emerging ITT programmes. The argument advanced here is that by so doing, a number of problems surrounding core skills would be resolved or lessened. They include the low status afforded to these units, especially those that are not assessed; the awkward distinction made between mandatory and optional units; and the uncertainty concerning the notion of transferability. Moreover, such a development might go some way towards combating any narrowly behaviourist, reductivist curriculum and generating greater confidence as to the merit of the work undertaken in vocational units.

7

Records of Achievement – Rhetoric or Reality?

Rob Halsall

INTRODUCTION

The contradictory nature of government policy on education and training as illustrated by the dual concerns to advocate vocational routes and to defend the existing A-level system is, in one sense, mirrored in the debate surrounding Records of Achievement (RoAs). Many of the arguments for introducing RoAs sprang from a critique of the domination of external examinations certification procedures and from a recognition of the ways in which recording achievement could constitute a powerful mechanism for responding to the post-Fordist economy. Here, foundation learning four of the National Training and Education Targets has particular relevance: education and training provision to develop self-reliance, flexibility and breadth. Government legislation has acknowledged the importance of RoAs in relation to this target but has also protected the external dimension in certification procedures. Here, we can note the reduced weighting afforded to GCSE coursework and the pressure to increase the external examination element in General National Vocational Qualifications (GNVQs). Certainly, Broadfoot's view of a decade ago that, 'it appears that England and Wales are now on the brink of an assessment revolution...major structural changes in...policy developments have begun to erode this longstanding acceptance of the desirability of external examinations' (1986:1) was somewhat precipitous. Moreover, there are in any case a number of tensions inherent to RoAs. These will be visited later in this chapter.

RECENT DEVELOPMENTS IN RECORDS OF ACHIEVEMENT

In July 1984 the DES expressed a wish for more work on RoAs and published a policy statement which indicated that all school leavers should be given one by the end of the decade (DES, 1984). This was influenced chiefly by a number of 'grassroots mission' developments that had taken off in the 1970s and early 1980s and which had laid down and proselytised a set of principles for RoAs (for example, Stansbury, 1980). Then, in December 1984, the DES announced financial support for nine pilot schemes covering 22 LEAs, to be overseen by a Records of Achievement National Steering Committee (RANSC) and to be the subject of evaluation by a team based jointly at Bristol University and the Open University. Although not directly funded by the DES, other important schemes also became established, many of which represented consortia activity of partnerships between one or more LEAs and Examining Boards. These included the Northern and the Cambridge Partnerships for Records of Achievement.

Several writers had suggested that RoAs had great potential for bringing about change in schools. Thus, Burgess and Adams (1986:76) stated that, 'It is potentially the most important national initiative in education since the establishment of a national system of public examination'. This view was supported by the final report of the Pilot Records of Achievement in Schools Evaluation, PRAISE (1988:178), which suggested that 'records of achievement pose a challenge to schools and teachers that is perhaps unprecedented in formal education', and Pole (1993:3) felt able to claim that by the end of the 1980s, 'the rhetoric of records of achievement as the bringers of change in schools was well established'.

In February 1991 the Secretaries of State for Education and Employment jointly launched a pilot National Record of Achievement (NRA) shortly followed by Circular 14/92 which required that all school leavers have, as from 1995, a summative NRA which would include several mandatory sections relating to different types of achievement. Extensive guidance notes for teachers concerning the NRA were then published by the National Council for Vocational Qualifications. This documentation was notable for the attention it paid to the processes underlying the production of the record: to recording achievement rather than simply the record itself, to the formative rather than just the summative aspect of schemes. It is in relation to the recording of achievement, as against the document *per se*, that the more powerful arguments for RoAs have been advanced.

WHY RECORDS OF ACHIEVEMENT?

Various writers have suggested reasons why record of achievement schemes should be pursued. One of these is a 'negative' argument, namely that RoAs can serve as some sort of antidote 'compensating for the disadvantages and limitations of...external exams' (Broadfoot, 1986:2). These include their inability to measure more than a small sample of achievements, their encouragement of extrinsic rather than intrinsic motivation, their norm-referenced nature and their concealment, through aggregated grading, of differences between various kinds of competence that have been acquired. More positively, it has been argued that RoAs can serve an integrative function in relation to the curriculum and assessment, recording and reporting, not least because they can help place assessment at the centre of the learning process where it is used as an aid to the diagnosis of student needs and as a basis for informing curriculum decisions (e.g. Mortimore and Keane, 1986; RANSC, 1989). RoAs can also help teachers manage learning through the use of teacher–student discussions, self-appraisal and recording of progress.

It has also been suggested that RoAs provide end-users with a more comprehensive and individualised record of students' achievements and that in so doing they can prove useful to employers and course providers in their selection procedures. Certainly, concern has been expressed by employers that educational institutions give insufficient attention to the relevance of their curricula to the world of work. In particular, it is claimed that skills required in everyday work situations are not being developed sufficiently. Most often cited are those relating to communication, problem solving, self-reliability, critical evaluation and collaboration. Accordingly, an increasing number of employers, usually from large enterprises, are looking towards RoAs for evidence of such skills (e.g. Berkeley, 1992). At the same time, RoAs can help students to be better equipped to present themselves for selection and interview for jobs, training and education. This aim has been a central concern of the northern-based Recording Achievement and Higher Education Project which has stimulated and supported considerable work regarding the thoughtful use by higher education applicants of their RoAs and action plans in completing UCAS forms and/or attending interviews.

As regards other direct benefits for students, most teachers who are enthusiastically involved in RoAs consistently mention their role in boosting students' motivation and commitment to their education. This can result from greater understanding of the purposes behind their work and assessment procedures and of what precisely is expected of them; from a focus on achievements rather than failures whereby opportunities are provided for students to experience and enjoy success, thus leading to enhanced self-confidence and self-esteem; and from the use of realistic target setting which can generate a sense of being in control, to some extent, of what happens to them.

Of all the arguments advanced in support of RoAs, however, possibly the most powerful is that they encourage student-centredness. This view is most comprehensively and forcefully articulated by Munby (1989). His book rests on the notion that good education is based on a set of values, the most fundamental of which is a belief in the desirability of a student-centred approach towards learning. For Munby, such an approach involves believing that students are unique individuals with different needs, experiences and feelings; that teachers should be concerned about students as 'whole' persons and not just about their academic needs; that there should be an emphasis on the processes necessary for effective learning; and that students should be given some responsibility for their own learning. This last point which relates to the development of more autonomous learners has been afforded particular prominence in the literature on RoAs. Here it is useful to rehearse the arguments put forward concerning this aim and to explore the relevance of RoAs to it.

Knowles (1981) has suggested that traditional education has been based on the premise that the central purpose of education is to produce knowledgeable persons who have concepts and skills required to function well in the world as it is now, and that this is possibly appropriate in a relatively stable world where people can function for the rest of their lives on the basis of their earlier learning. However, the world is not stable. Knowledge and skills have an increasingly short life. In this context, an alternative assumption about the purpose of education is that it is to produce autonomous lifelong learners. If so, then the main mission must be the development of the skills of autonomous learning rather than the acquisition of content. There are various views on the nature of these skills but there is considerable consensus that they include:

● diagnosing one's own learning needs;

- formulating one's own learning objectives/setting learning targets;
- identifying for oneself necessary resources to achieve these;
- taking the initiative in the use of those resources;
- assessing one's progress and achievements;
- identifying and providing evidence as to these.

In short, the argument is that the emphasis in education must be on the processes of learning. This is not to negate the importance of content; indeed, the acquisition of content (as against its transmission) is an important result of the learning process, i.e. content is more important as an outcome rather than as an input. A number of significant national initiatives have sought to further the development of autonomous learning, for example the Technical and Vocational Initiative in schools and colleges and Enterprise in Higher Education. But why consider RoAs in relation to the development of autonomous learning?

At this point it is necessary to articulate more clearly the central processes of recording achievement. They can be seen as those identified in the NRA guidance for teachers: reviewing and action-planning, the latter comprising goal-setting, target-setting and the identification of arrangements that need to be made to achieve targets. Reviewing leads to identification of achievements to date and of current strengths and needs, based on reflection upon learning activities. It is the starting point for action-planning and it also provides opportunities for the sharing of learning objectives for programmes of study and for the student and teacher to compare their perceptions of the teaching and learning experience. Building on the reviewing process, action-planning helps students to maximise their abilities and opportunities, whether within a programme of study or at a transition point. The first step is to set goals. These might be short, medium or longer term. Where action-planning is being used within programmes of study they are likely to be detailed and short term. In managing transition they may be more general in nature. To reach goals their requirements need to be understood and learning needs must be identified, learning targets being an expression of these needs. It is this context of goal and target-setting within programmes of study wherein lies the importance of student understanding of course aims and requirements. Once targets have been set, the learner needs to identify ways in which they can be met:

decide on what arrangements must be made to satisfy the learning needs. This will often involve gaining access to resources of one sort or another.

To return, then, to the potential of recording achievement. Reflection on learning and review of progress are central to the setting of achievable and relevant goals and to the assessment of the effectiveness of actions. Action planning addresses the setting of achievable and relevant goals and involves learners not only in negotiating what it is they need to learn but also in making arrangements for that learning to occur. There are few more direct measures of active engagement in the learning process or of responsibility, accountability, empowerment and performance than being centrally involved in reflection on one's learning, in identifying future goals and learning needs and, indeed, in marshalling evidence to testify to one's achievements: in other words, than in being involved in recording achievement.

Notwithstanding all of these perceived benefits from RoAs, however, two questions must be raised. First, what actual evidence is there of RoAs generating such outcomes? Second, do RoAs represent a two-edged sword: is there a 'downside'? The following two sections seek to address these questions.

THE EVIDENCE

To what extent is involvement in RoAs based on enthusiastic belief rather than firm evidence as to the benefits? For example, what evidence is there regarding their integrative function, increased motivation and improved self-esteem, more active engagement in the learning process, greater success with job and HE applications and the provision of more useful information to end-users? There is much in the way of anecdote and there is a wealth of favourable opinions offered by enthusiastic teachers, but empirical data is scarce. Where there is data it rarely provides unequivocal evidence to suggest that the alleged benefits of RoAs have materialised. Here, though, it is necessary to point out that much of the evidence dates back to the late eighties and does not take account of developments since then, especially those in the context of the NRA. No further work on the same scale as the PRAISE report has been published, but what more recent evidence there is does not appear to alter significantly the conclusion drawn above.

Integrative?

In terms of their integrative function, the PRAISE Report (1988:103) noted that the development of RoAs had, in fact, gone hand in hand with curriculum review and development and in particular had prompted 'the beginnings of movement towards the erosion of the traditional divide between pastoral and academic aspects of the curriculum'. However, there seemed to be less success as regards developments in recording progress. The authors remarked upon the way in which diversity had characterised the nature of recording documents used by different departments, approaches to the recording process by different teachers and development strategies used by different tutorial or departmental teams, all of which suggested a diversity in underlying assessment principles. Although it was observed that schools had felt a need for whole-school assessment policies to integrate the assessment principles informing a number of curriculum initiatives, such as the GCSE and the TVEI, and were aware that RoAs held the potential to provide that integrating function, 'Few of our case study schools attempted to formulate a whole-school assessment policy, and those that did discovered that the course was not smooth' (PRAISE, 1988:66).

Nevertheless, the PRAISE authors did go on to say that they expected something in the nature of an assessment policy to emerge in the near future in most of their case study institutions. Although it is not possible to say whether or not a policy did eventually emerge in these institutions, available data points to a mixed picture elsewhere. Pole's (1993:135) study is based on one school only where he identified 'a gap between the rhetoric of what the Head and several other staff would like to believe was happening and the school implementation of the Record of Achievement process'. Here, evidence seemed to belie claims of a recording and reporting system which was integrated with the curriculum and had major implications for the way in which teachers approached their jobs. Pupils did not appear to see ROAs as a holistic process and staff generally viewed them as 'a series of tasks to be conducted rather than an ongoing process' (Pole, 1993:188).

However, the author has had the opportunity to investigate RoAs in a variety of institutions in the role of external verifier for the Manchester Metropolitan University's Recording Achievement Accreditation scheme. In the course of this activity several examples of excellent practice have been observed as regards the integrative function of RoAs. To quote from two accreditation reports:

> Recording of achievement is clearly a central and integrative strategy in respect of several major school aims such as the development of an achievement-orientated and caring school ethos, the development of subject teaching-learning practices, and the development of self-confident youngsters with a positive self-image. (The Manchester Metropolitan University, 1993b)

> The curriculum area is to be applauded for the way in which individual action planning, reviewing and core skills are integrated into recording achievement. ROA and assessment are also fully-integrated activities and students have a good understanding both of assessment demands and criteria. (The Manchester Metropolitan University, 1994)

Of course, it must be noted that these reports relate to self-selected institutions in that they put themselves forward for accreditation, but nevertheless they do provide some support for the optimism of the PRAISE authors in relation to the future development of assessment policies.

End-users

Have RoAs provided end-users with more comprehensive records and has this been helpful in selection procedures? Have they helped students to better present themselves for selection and interview? Here, there are two major sources of evidence: evaluation of the pilot NRA (Research International, 1993) which focused on its use in selection by employers, training organisations (TOs) and post-16 colleges, and evaluation of the Recording Achievement and Higher Education Project (Hustler et al., 1994a). Although the NRA study involved random sampling of end-users, data analysis related only to those institutions actually using NRAs for selection purposes. Of the institutions that provided information, nearly two-thirds of employers, nearly one-third of TOs and two-fifths of colleges did not use the NRA. This itself does not present a very heartening picture. In relation to the institutions that did use it and that responded to requests for information – 92 employers, 90 TOs and 156 college staff – the proportions of interviews with applicants showing their NRA were 40% for employers and college staff and 27% for TOs, though only 14% of selectors overall had taken an NRA into consideration before the interview stage. Of those who responded to the question, 71% of employers and about three-fifths of TOs and college staff thought that the NRA was very good or good at painting a picture of applicants, especially in relation to their personal skills. The two most helpful components of the NRA were seen as the qualifications page and the personal statement, the latter being seen as particularly useful in that it offered extra information not available through other items. The report concluded that:

> there is considerable enthusiasm for the NRA. Use is mainly within interviews...and it is considered useful, helpful and 'truthful'. Interviewers think it paints a good picture of the individual, providing real insights, perhaps especially through the personal statement. (Research International, 1993:24)

While this is an encouraging comment it could also be seen as somewhat 'rose-tinted' given the proportions of institutions that did not use the NRA at all and the fairly minimal use of it at the applications stage. The NRA evaluation also included interviews with 208 16-year-old students who had finished compulsory schooling in 1992 and who had been involved in the pilot NRA. Again, the data is not totally reassuring. Whilst the item most commonly used by these students in making applications for employment, training or further education was the NRA, over one-third did not use the document. Of these, almost half did not do so because it did not occur to them to use it. The report commented:

> use of the NRA could have been more widespread. Lack of school support and guidance could, perhaps, account for this, since a significant group of young people did not even think of using it, especially at the application stage. (Research International, 1993:35)

In fact, almost half of the students commented that they had never been given help while at school on how best to use the NRA in applications. However, more students had taken the NRA to interviews, this decision being mainly their own, though some had been asked to take it; 40% and 13% of those being interviewed at colleges and for jobs respectively. Furthermore, three-quarters of those who took their NRA to interview reported that it had been used by the interviewer and most of these students felt that it gave a good picture of themselves and had impressed the interviewer. Also, almost two-thirds of these students had found the NRA useful in preparing for, and during, their interviews, and here, 'it is apparent that young people who completed the NRA themselves or together with their tutors, had a much higher opinion of its usefulness than those whose tutors filled it in for them' (Research International, 1993:33).

Whilst the NRA evaluation focused upon applications and selection at 16, the evaluation of the Recording Achievement and Higher Education Project focused upon the role of RoAs in applying to higher education institutions. The furtherance of this role was a central thrust within the Project and the evaluators identified several positive outcomes relating to this aim. Thus, there was:

> A productive process of 'enlightenment' for many HE participants, who gained a clearer insight into the development, compilation and use of RoA...improved access for LEA, school and college representatives to individual course selection criteria...which has assisted in focused RoA action planning and informed the content of the 'additional information section' on the UCAS form. (Hustler *et al.*, 1994:46)

There were also important outcomes such as the production of guidance materials on the use of RoAs in the HE admissions process which point in particular to the use of personal statements and action plans, the inclusion of institutional statements on the use of RoAs at the admissions point in HEI prospectuses and the development of policies within some HEIs which clarified their stance on the use of RoAs. The evaluators also noted that 'It is significant that LEA representatives report the increased interest in RoA at the post-16 phase as a direct result of the incentive it provides as a tool for application to HE' (Hustler *et al.*, 1994a:47). However, the report concluded that there was:

> An acknowledgement by participants from both sectors of the restricted potential for the use of RoA within the admissions processes of courses which do not interview candidates (and that) some limited exploration of the use of RoA within interviews...revealed very mixed responses to their value and effectiveness within admissions, as a result of either a lack of HE tutor training in respect of the use of the document in the interview, or a lack of quality in the RoA presented by the candidate. (Hustler *et al.*, 1994a:46)

Certainly, it appears to be the case that the greatest potential for RoAs in selection for higher education courses seems to be in their judicious use at the applications stage, especially through drawing upon students' personal statements and action plans both for deciding which courses to apply for and in (re)writing a personal statement for section 10 of the UCAS form. This point might also be germane to applications for jobs, training and further education.

Attitudes

Regarding the role of RoAs in boosting students' motivation, self-confidence and self-esteem, most of the available evidence comes from the PRAISE report, though its authors comment that, 'this report consistently reiterates how hard it is to detect changes in pupil attitude that can be directly linked to records of achievement' (PRAISE, 1988:158). Nevertheless, they proceed to cite most of the pilot scheme reports as suggesting that there had been some improvement in pupils' attitudes, especially where they had been encouraged to take responsibility for their own learning and had been involved in reviewing and assessment. Thus, the Wigan pilot report stated that 'some schools have observed that the pupils are becoming more confident and "able to challenge" often in a very mature manner....This is directly attributed to the recording of achievement' (PRAISE, 1988:121).

The PRAISE report also observed that there were indications that helping to make pupils aware of their learning targets and involving them in self-assessment and dialogue with teachers led to greater student self-esteem and motivation, referring to:

> evidence that many pupils have found the opportunity of talking with their teachers on a one-to-one basis about their achievements, experiences, needs and appropriate future targets a rewarding and helpful experience that has had a positive effect on their motivation....Pupils' motivation is significantly improved to the extent that they are given responsibility for their learning and are involved in reviewing and assessment. (PRAISE, 1988:158–59)

However, it must be said that using internal reports from the pilot schemes themselves as data is not unproblematic. Moreover, several of the pilot scheme reports indicated that many students were *demotivated* by formative recording where this involved extensive writing and that some were bored with self-assessment. It was also noted that some students developed negative attitudes as a result of feeling themselves to be under constant scrutiny.

Autonomous learners?

Finally, to what extent has involvement in RoAs led students to be more purposeful and autonomous learners? The PRAISE report noted that establishing any such causal link is even more problematic than is the case with student attitudes, but went on to say that:

> Overall…our evidence documents many teachers who have been favourably impressed by changes in both attitude and achievement which they attribute to records of achievement. Equally some of the pupils we studied felt the provision of clearer objectives, personal targets and more supportive relationships with teachers had enabled them to make more progress than would otherwise have been the case. (PRAISE, 1988:162)

However, the sort of data this statement rests on is problematic: it represents little more than anecdotal evidence. Certainly, there is no attempt to measure achievement or progress whether related or not to involvement in RoAs. Based on sounder evidence are the authors' conclusions that, 'pupils in our case study schools have grown in self-awareness and in their ability to reflect more accurately on their academic progress and personal development' (PRAISE, 1988:40), but Pole's study of Benton School can be interpreted as a counter to the above. For example, he found that whilst claims have been made about the importance of target setting to the recording of achievement process, pupils did not give great attention to their identified goals, many were unable to recall them and saw target setting as an isolated event to which they did not attach much importance. The PRAISE report itself revealed difficulties in the processes of reviewing and negotiation, referring to one evaluation study of a college where staff reported that some students found these processes:

> threatening and bewildering. They commented that students had been overwhelmed by the one-to-one review and diffident about negotiating comments….Some found that conducting the review with students had been tedious and unproductive….It is not easy to get students to comment fruitfully. (PRAISE, 1988:123)

None of this is intended to suggest that involvement in recording achievement cannot contribute to the development of more autonomous learners; indeed, the Manchester Metropolitan University accreditation activity has provided glimpses of such in the context of its 'self-selected' institutions. Thus, from the report on North Manchester High School for Girls:

> Considerable support is given to the youngsters in recording and reviewing their progress...and in target setting for further development...although there is this support, it is also the case that a significant degree of responsibility is invested in, and taken on board by, the youngsters. It is *their* responsibility to set targets, to reflect on progress, to produce personal statements. That they view such activities as normal, 'easy' and non-threatening is testimony to the success of RoA practices within the school. (The Manchester Metropolitan University, 1993b)

However, as with all of the other claimed outcomes of RoAs we must regard the jury as still out. Clearly, much more research is needed in this area.

TENSIONS

Broadfoot (1986:67) wrote a decade ago that, 'Amid the euphoria currently being generated by the realisation that records of achievement are really on the policy agenda, there is also widespread realisation, that many of the issues raised by this innovation are deeply significant', and went on to post a warning note, 'lest in our enthusiasm for change we fail to notice the flaws that, unchecked, could turn the dream into a nightmare'.

In particular, three interrelated issues have been the subject of some concern: privacy, ownership and control. RoAs may be seen as a continuous scrutiny of all aspects of the life and work of students whereby teachers have been taken into the niches of students' lives that had been the concern of family, community and faith. It is not out of the question that such 'surveillance' might have opposite effects to those which advocates of RoAs desire. The threat of intrusion could cause some students to ignore the system or play the system by presenting what they think teachers want them to present. For some it could even exacerbate existing negative self-concepts. This could be the case in particular where information relates to emotions and details about family life and, as mentioned in the previous section, the PRAISE report noted that some students developed negative attitudes to RoAs because they saw themselves to be under constant scrutiny.

There is a fine line between demanding such information and making students aware of the potential relevance of that sort of data to their record. There are issues here to do with the dangers of misusing access to information and with the possibility of imposing school-based value judgements on it. We can too easily assume that interest in out-of-school involvements is a legitimate extension of the influence of the school, albeit underscored with benign intentions to support learning and celebrate a wide range of achievements. In my own experience as an external verifier of record of achievement systems, concerns relating to RoAs as 'surveillance' have most often come from black and Asian students. Is this more than coincidence?

Now, as a counter to the above, it can be argued that whatever information is contained in records is owned by the students. Most institutions make much of this but the concept of ownership is fraught with problems. RoAs are not purely private documents. For example, they are accessed by staff for review purposes and for updating information. Many institutions store either the document itself or a copy. Furthermore, the documents are designed for use with external audiences and this might make it impossible for students to retain total control over the nature of usage. These points in turn could constrain individuals regarding the nature of the information to be recorded. Will they feel secure enough to disclose truthfully their private wishes and needs, or will they feel a need to manage and manipulate the information to be offered? If so, how do they and staff deal with the ethical issues raised?

The matter of ownership is, of course, inextricably linked with that of control and this concept needs to be considered in relation to those of student-centredness and empowerment. As explored earlier, RoAs are seen by many people as creating an opportunity for placing students at the centre of their own learning, for example by giving them greater responsibility for their own assessment and by empowering them with the ability to chart their own development paths. However, as Hargreaves (1986:214) has pointed out:

> The personal record component of records of achievement also has an extraordinary capacity to restrict young peoples' individuality, to discipline and control them through the power of a pervasive and intrusive pattern of personal assessment...bound up with a more generalised trend towards the development and implementation of

increasingly sophisticated techniques of social surveillance within society at large.

Hargreaves draws on Foucault's (1977) notions of normalisation and hierarchy (1977). The former involves comparing and differentiating people in relation to assumed norms of what is desirable. The latter involves a process whereby power is not only exercised through control by observation but where the powerful, the observers, are not seen to be observing. Foucault saw all types of examinations, including case record assessment, as a process embodying these notions and Hargreaves draws a comparison between aspects of the formative process of recording personal achievements and Foucault's example of an extended case record which can be retrieved and referred to when institutional guidance, control and correction is felt necessary.

In response to such analysis, advocates of RoAs can argue that they represent an attack on norm-referenced attainment, that they employ non-hierarchical elements of partnership and negotiation and that students control the use of summative statements in relation to end-users. However, is it not the case that expectations by teachers and end-users concerning the sorts of information to be found in RoAs can constitute a different form of norm-referencing? Here Stronach's (1989:167–68) analysis of a personal statement within a record of achievement is illustrative of how:

> The narrative covers, but cannot obscure, the underlying and *a priori* categories (quietness, activity, risk-taking, leadership, example to others, cooperativeness). It is a piece of directed writing. Nor can it disguise its normative rather than ipsative nature (usually, quite, good, always, quite a lot, never). Any...negotiations invite self-scaling by the learner and reduces educational dialogue to a discussion of these implicit gradings...it also comprises a social assessment.

Also, can there be an equal partnership between teacher and student and, in particular, is negotiation conducted between people who not only are partners with equal powers but actually see themselves as such? The sort of transcript analysis of reviewing processes carried out by James (1989) suggests that often this is not the case. Here, the teacher set the pace and tone of the one-to-one interviews, imposed her own assessment when there were disagreements and reinforced 'occasions when the student's self-assessment agrees with her own'.

Finally, can students really be in control of their RoAs when pressures surround them to share information with others who they know to be in a more powerful position than themselves, often people who control their immediate, and possibly long-term, destinies? This surely applies to their use with end-users such as employers and HE providers, but also with teachers. As Pole (1993:126) observed:

> At Benton School pupils were informed of their rights to restrict access to the Record of Achievement and were asked to give written permission to allow the head to use it....Refusal to do so may have resulted in bad feeling...and...the pupil could not be sure of the kind or format of alternative information which would have been made available to employers and other users. Giving permission was probably the easiest path for the pupil to take even if he or she had reservations about it.

And, of course, not only can the use of RoAs be seen by students as essentially mandatory, but their very existence is compulsory as is student engagement in such processes as negotiation and reviewing. The question could be asked: where lies the notions of empowerment and autonomy here?

CONCLUDING COMMENTS

This chapter has argued that what evidence exists concerning RoAs does not suggest that they have delivered the sorts of outcomes that were signalled by their advocates, at least not on any significant scale, although clearly there are notable exceptions in this or that institution. It has also noted a number of concerns and tensions surrounding RoAs that can be viewed as constituting a critique, though it is important to note that this critique does emanate from a period prior to the implementation of the NRA when profiles were at least as much the focus as were records of achievement. These were, moreover, often associated with particular schemes, many of which were targeted at lower achievers, e.g. the Certificate of Pre-Vocational Education and Youth Training Schemes, and which were invariably dominated by fragmentary outcome statements and simple 'tick box' frameworks. It is also the case that although they spelled out the possible 'nightmare scenario', most of the contributors to the critique of RoAs did accept that they contained the potential for realising the sorts of benefits outlined earlier in this chapter and accepted that the negative aspects could be avoided. As Hargreaves (1986:219) commented, 'the nightmarish Orwellian vision...in which...all means of escape from the all-encompassing gaze of permanent observation and assessment have been removed...is not by any means inevitable'.

Teachers, though, will need to be aware of the thin dividing line between 'care and control, independence and surveillance' (Hargreaves, 1986:220), and take care to both embrace record of achievement systems which avoid control and surveillance and work to achieve the potential benefits. Here, it is essential that the quality assurance of RoAs is taken seriously. This has been identified as a key issue since the 1984 policy statement on records of achievement which contained reference to the need for national currency and accreditation. As Burgess and Adams (1986:83) stated, 'The Secretary of State recognised that there should be as much assurance as possible about the currency, reliability and significance of the information in the records'.

However, in line with the increased emphasis on the formative role of RoAs there is more lately a concern for quality assurance regarding the learning processes. Thus, Berkeley (1992:5) writing as Manager of Education and Careers of Rover Group believed that:

The success of the NRA as the accepted means of helping to empower individuals to take more ownership of their own learning and development can be said to rely crucially on it being the product of a consistent process.

Also, as I (Halsall, 1994:23) have written, albeit in the context of recording achievement in higher education, 'Credibility relates not only to the authenticity of achievements and experiences contained in the RoA, but more important to the genuineness of the formative, learning process involved in its production'.

The NRA initiative did not attempt to establish a national quality assurance system for RoAs but suggested that the Investors in People (IIP) initiative, initially devised to address the training and development needs of employees, would transfer comfortably to the implementation of the NRA in schools. Although there has been considerable interest by schools in IIP, relatively few record of achievement schemes have fallen within its orbit to date. Most schools and, indeed, colleges which have paid attention to the matter of quality assurance have done so in the context of accreditation systems which became established by the late 1980s. On the whole, these have been developed and operated by individual, or consortia of, local education authorities, often in partnership with Training and Enterprise Councils or Examining Boards, though there are some recent exceptions including the Manchester Metropolitan University's recording achievement accreditation scheme.

The key accreditation criteria that have been consistently adopted and applied in these quality assurance systems are those which relate to the learning process. They also address the need to integrate recording achievement with broader learning and assessment practices and the need to develop appropriate skills on the part of students and staff. For example:

> How involved are the students in sharing assessment criteria and recording achievement...what time (is) set aside for reviewing and target-setting....How is the ROA system integrated into (school assessment) policy? (Manchester LEA, 1992)

> The school/college should encourage students to acquire and practise skills that promote their responsibility as learners...is expected to design the nature and delivery of its curriculum so that students are involved in planning and reviewing their learning...reviewing and recording attainments and achievements should be as an integral part of the learning process...opportunities should be provided for the development and practise of appropriate skills, so that all those involved can take increased responsibility for their own learning. (OCEA, 1992)

However, three points need to be made concerning the quality assurance of RoAs. First, it is one thing for accreditation schemes to be in place but it is another to be sure that the criteria they use are consistent with each other and that they are being rigorously applied. Second, only self-selected institutions are subject to quality assurance. In relation to these points it can be argued that the NRA initiative fell short in not attempting to establish a national quality system, or at least in not insisting that all institutions engage with record of achievement quality assurance schemes which in turn would be subject to national kitemarking. Third, any criteria that were to be consistently and rigorously applied would need to take into account the arguments presented in the critique of RoAs by capturing the need to prevent control and surveillance from subverting care and independence. It is not at all clear that existing schemes succeed in this.

In addition to the above, a number of other conditions need to be met if RoAs are to realise their potential. Quality assurance criteria could take into account some, but not all, of these. In particular, RoAs need to be an integral part of institutional development plans and of whole-institution policies on teaching–learning, guidance and assessment, reporting and recording. There is also a particular need to co-ordinate RoAs and action planning and the processes that support them. There needs to be a commitment to recording achievement by the vast majority of staff, not least by senior managers who must commit the necessary resources including appropriate infrastructures. There is also a need for end-user confidence in, and support for, the quality of the product and of the processes underlying it and, related to this, it is essential that there is cross-sectoral development of RoAs. Here, there are issues concerning continuity and progression.

How, for example, is continuity to be ensured between successive phases, e.g. 11–14, 14–16 and 16+, and between different sectors, e.g. schools, colleges, HEIs and employment? Personnel in different phases or sectors will need to develop a shared understanding of the nature and purposes of RoAs. Activity in successive phases and sectors needs to be planned so as to ensure the ever-deepening of learning processes and reinforcement of the skills of autonomous learning. There is a powerful argument for extensive cross-phase and multi-sector networking such as that provided by the Recording Achievement and Higher Education Project. Of course, as that project has discovered, it is unlikely that identical ways can be adopted in approaching and managing RoAs: there are different cultures and organisational features across the sectors and due note must be taken of these as simple replication in one context of what happens in another is unlikely to arise or to be successful. Network members need to be sensitive to the varied circumstances that pertain in different contexts. However, where this sensitivity exists, networking can be a highly positive force.

All of this represents a considerable challenge but it is one that needs to be grasped if the benefits of ROAs are to be realised on a far greater scale than hitherto and if the pitfalls are to be avoided.

8

Rationales for Student-Centred Learning

David Hustler and Phil Hodkinson

A SHARED COMMITMENT?

Across a number of communities and networks involved in post-14 education, there seems to be considerable consensus regarding the appropriateness of certain types of teaching and learning styles, which in turn are seen as associated with certain principles to do with learner empowerment. Vocabularies vary, of course, as does the degree of precision with which distinctions are or are not made between descriptors such as teaching 'style' and teaching 'method'. The vocabulary includes active learning, student-centred learning, negotiated learning, co-operative learning, flexible learning and learning through doing. In terms of specific emphases we find varying priority given to student choice, student negotiation, self-assessment or student decision-making. People commonly talk of teaching and learning methodologies through which students take more responsibility for their own learning, albeit within different degrees of structuring and the overarching parameters for this. As shorthand for this set of educational methodologies or practices, the term 'student-centred learning' will be used.

Each of the above terms and phrases can be connected with extensive and rapidly developing literatures and, more usefully perhaps, overviews of these (e.g. Boud, 1981; Barnes, 1989; Entwistle, 1992; Kyriacou, 1992; Tomlinson and Kilner, 1991). It is worth noting that these references cover differing educational sectors – schools, further education (FE) and higher education (HE) – and this establishes, at least to some extent, that learner autonomy and 'student-centred learning' are on the agenda across the variety of institutions concerned with 14+ education. On occasion this literature is explicitly associated with particular funded initiatives and national projects. Barnes (1989) is concerned with 'active learning' related to the Technical and Vocational Educational Initiative (TVEI), focusing especially at that time on the 14–16 secondary school context. Tomlinson and Kilner (1991) discuss the theoretical bases informing the Flexible Learning Development Project where the major initiatives took place within both the upper age ranges of secondary schools and FE. Entwistle (1992) relates primarily to the HE context and in particular to the Enterprise in Higher Education (EHE) developments.

Interestingly the three major initiatives referred to here were funded through the Employment Department, not the Department for Education (DfE), or its forerunner, the Department of Education and Science (DES). Also worth recognising is that the Employment Department has continued to fund a range of projects where student-centred learning is an important theme. Recent examples include the Recording Achievement and Higher Education project operating across 15 HE Institutions and 11 Local Education Authorities and associated schools and colleges (Hustler *et al.*, 1994a), and the current Guidance and Learner Autonomy projects focusing on HE Institutions (Hustler *et al.*, 1994b). We point to this constellation of Employment Department associated projects here, because not only are the themes related to student-centred learning similar in many respects, but some of the personnel associated with these different projects can be regarded as forming a community, or at least a coalition, who interrelate through various formal and informal networks. Acknowledging important distinctions within the literature and across different projects, it is possible to identify certain shared commitments. The purpose of this chapter is to raise questions about the sources of, and bases for, some of these. In doing this we should emphasise that we are raising questions about commitments which we hold and believe we share with others.

A recurring theme in the literature is the notion of students taking more control of their own learning. Kyriacou (1992:310–11), in a discussion of active learning in the context of secondary school mathematics, characterises it in essence as:

> the use of learning activities where pupils are given a marked degree of ownership and control over the learning activities used, where the learning experience is open-ended rather than tightly predetermined, and where the pupil is able to actively participate and shape the learning experience.

Entwistle (1992:4), primarily focusing on the HE context, talks of 'the emphasis is on arranging classroom settings and activities to encourage a variety of forms of learning, and allowing pupils more control over their activities'. Both of these authors tie back to the work of Barnes (1989) where he systematises the principles associated with active learning within TVEI, as does Baddely in his overview of teachers and learners sharing planning and negotiating activities (Hustler *et al.*, 1991). Interestingly this last publication drew primarily on work by teachers and schools within the Lower Attaining Pupils Project (LAPP) during the early 1980s and prior to the Education Reform Act, a project initiated by Sir Keith Joseph which was DES funded and which some schools are now revisiting in the light of the latest National Curriculum changes. In the literature we find recurring use of the term 'empowerment' for students, with presumably considerable implications for 'conventional' relationships and for hierarchy. If we accept this shared commitment to help students take more control of their learning, then a good question is the simple one: why? Three rather different answers are offered, each of which leads to additional questions.

EMPOWERMENT, DEMOCRACY AND CITIZENSHIP

One set of arguments concerns the need to develop more 'democratic' forms of discourse within our educational system, sometimes presented as self-evidently important. It is to do with challenging false hierarchies and preparing young people to participate more fully in an active democracy. Relationships of deference and subordination are viewed as dangerous to democratic life. Arguments of this type are much more global in scope than some of the others which follow. Significant contributions have been made by the German critical thinker, Habermas (1978), radical Americans such as Giroux (1988) and McLaren (1989), and perhaps, above all, by the radical Brazilian educator, Paulo Friere (1972). In Britain, Stenhouse (1975) was highly influential, together with a number of educationists, projects and reports long associated with progressive ideologies, such as the Humanities Curriculum Project and the Plowden Report. The link with democracy is most clearly explicit in contributions to Harber and Meighan (1989). There are parallels here with the arguments of Kemmis (1983) and others within the action research movement, in terms of certain assumptions about what makes for appropriate teaching and learning experiences as well as what makes for effective teacher professionals. Hammersley (1993) provides an interesting and challenging critique of the 'teacher research' movement, where he centres on what he regards as the unexplicated commitments and assumptions associated with that movement.

One answer, then, about why we should adopt student-centred learning approaches draws primarily on what might be termed a democratising ideology. Fundamentally, it is about social justice. We are holding up this possible answer to ourselves as writers and also inviting you, the reader, to consider whether this is part of your answer. If it is, what evidence is there that 'student-centred learning' makes any contribution to democratisation processes? Or is this question about evidence misplaced? This last question is an important one to address. It can be argued, for example, that it is a student's right to have access to student-centred learning practices, as part of any education system which has autonomy or self-actualisation as a key purpose (Hodkinson, 1994). More generally, it is well worth asking what might be meant by 'evidence' in this context and elsewhere, as well as whether a search for evidence is or is not appropriate.

No thinkers of substance argue that student-centred learning is alone sufficient to democratise and liberate young people. Indeed, critics of such approaches, such as Avis (1991b), would argue that if pedagogy alone is seen as fulfilling this role, the result may be to reduce empowerment rather than enhance it – a line of argument we will return to later. What is argued, rather, is that student-centred learning is an important element of democratic education, provided other conditions are also met.

MEANINGFUL AND EFFECTIVE LEARNING

A second answer draws primarily on the works of psychologists and others who see a positive association between more powerful learning experiences and outcomes and both the allocation of more active roles to learners and the establishment of more interactive relationships between teachers and learners. Once more, much of the original thinking of this type comes from outside Britain. Perhaps the most influential has been the work of two Americans, Rogers (1969) and Kolb (1983). A slightly different route to similar pedagogical conclusions, comes from studies of the long-standing failures of more traditional educational provision, in America (Brause, 1992), Australia (Bloomer et al., 1992) and Britain (Brandes and Ginnis, 1986). From within the British context, both Entwistle (1992) and Tomlinson and Kilner (1991) overview the work of a number of theorists supporting this position. Reference can be found to the close relationship between 'deep learning' and 'self-regulated learning'. Linked with this answer is the theoretical support associated with authors such as Kolb (1983), where learning cycle models need to take account of differing learning styles. The implication here is that students need to be 'empowered', at least in the sense that they are helped to become aware of their own learning styles and opportunities are provided in relation to differing styles.

This carries implications for open-endedness and necessary stages of negotiation, with consequences, therefore, for any entrenched power relationships. Other parallels can be drawn in the British scene with the early work of Douglas Barnes (1976) on language and learning and the critique of 'transmission' teaching in terms of its lack of effectiveness regarding learning outcomes (because of the relative absence of meaningful learning experiences). There are also in this literature a variety of attempts to challenge certain ways of conceptualising curriculum 'knowledge' and some of these approaches draw on the early work of Michael Young and his fellow contributors (Young, 1971) concerning the relationships between knowledge and control. It is perhaps not too surprising that, as the National Curriculum developed, the DES and then the DfE rapidly disassociated itself from notions such as that of the 'negotiated curriculum' which is central to all student-centred approaches (Bloomer et al., 1992).

The answer here, then, is linked with the need to change pedagogy because there are positive consequences for effective learning. The question then becomes, in what senses are we taking 'effective learning' and what evidence is there relating to any of these senses? One of the answers connects with effective learning in terms of a longer term perspective to do with 'learning how to learn', 'life-long learning' etc. Here we connect closely with the core skills discussions found in Chapter 6. What sort of evidence is there in this area and what sort of evidence could we be looking for? There is, as Entwistle (1992) notes, a fair amount of anecdotal evidence concerning teachers' and students' perceptions regarding the effectiveness of 'student-centred learning'. This includes evaluation work done in the North West regarding perceptions of flexible learning approaches (Hustler and Roden, 1993), as well as numerous small studies associated with TVEI and EHE. In brief, people seem to feel it works.

Is this good enough? The same question might be posed, as in fact it has by Halsall in Chapter 7, of the effectiveness of involvement in recording achievement in relation to the many arguments concerning the crucial importance of reviewing and previewing processes to effective learning. Once again, what sort of evidence supports this? What sort of evidence could? What has not been made explicit are assertions about allocating more involvement to students, increased motivation, confidence and self-esteem and effective learning. Many view relationships between these as crucial. However, this is a problematic line to pursue because it can be difficult to escape the claim that arguments for 'student-centred learning' are more associated with its virtues for particular students and particular groupings: the lower attainers and the disadvantaged, i.e. those whom schooling primarily fails.

We should remind ourselves here of the old argument that educational innovations tend to be primarily associated with safe areas, with low-status areas and low-status people, where from some points of view it does not really matter. Not a few of the student-centred learning developments in Britain within the last 15 years have been associated with projects and initiatives concerned with low-status vocational curricula and 'less able' young people. Some of these, such as LAPP and the Certificate of Prevocational Education (CPVE) and even TVEI itself, have been relatively short-lived, marginal and, therefore, a safe area of experimentation (Hodkinson and Sparkes, 1993).

There are, though, some recent examples of student-centredness in higher status curriculum areas. Within both mathematics and science education, it is currently fashionable to focus teaching around a constructivist view of learning. In essence, the argument is that what any student learns depends, to a considerable extent, on the perceptions they already bring to the classroom (Howard, 1987). Thus, the argument goes, a prerequisite of successful teaching is the need to discover what students know and believe, in order to challenge misconceptions and build on strengths (Cobb, 1994; Driver *et al.*, 1994). The inescapable conclusion is that teaching must become student-centred, at least to a degree. In both science and mathematics, for example, much interesting work is currently being developed with cartoons (Keogh and Naylor, 1993, 1995) and games (Hatch and Shiu, 1992) respectively to ensure active discussion about the nature of scientific understanding.

EDUCATION, VOCATIONALISM AND THE WORLD OF WORK

A somewhat different set of answers is associated with the drive to break down the boundaries of traditional academe. At one level, this is captured in the TVEI and EHE emphases on the world of work, work-based learning and practical and experiential learning. There are implications here for weakening the boundaries between educational institutions (schools, colleges or universities) and broader communities, with consequences for the management of time and space for learning. Allowing students to engage with the 'real world' can perhaps be seen as allocating them more control, through the weakening of traditional teaching and learning boundaries. At other levels this is captured in what at times seem to be major disputes and differing agendas between the DfE and the Employment Department. It is not by chance that many of the networks and communities referred to earlier have received funding through the Employment Department. 'Student-centred learning' as a set of practices here is shaped by views on the needs of the economy and business and industrial communities. Once again, there are connections with the core skills arguments, with learning to learn and the need for a flexible labour force. Connections can also be drawn between the emphasis on learner autonomy and analysis of Ball et al., (1991) of the conditions for effective and lifelong learning in a learning society. What emerges here is a curious alliance between progressives and certain sections of government.

Jamieson (1985) was one of the first to identify this paradox. The drive to vocationalism was part of the movement triggered by then Prime Minister James Callaghan's 'Great Debate' in 1976. Simultaneously, progressive and student-centred teaching was attacked, whilst relevance to industry and employment was praised. Yet, as industry, government departments and educationists responded to the latter, it was student-centred approaches that developed. Jamieson explained that this was because of the assumptions by British industrialists that 'real' learning was learning by doing. Most recently, this can be seen in the current emphasis on 'work based learning', in the developing system of National Vocational Qualifications (NVQs) and elsewhere. Jamieson raised the fundamental question, further explored here, as to whether industry-related vocational developments in Britain were examples of institutional hegemony (possibly leading to repression) or pedagogical liberation.

For Avis (1991b), the former was clearly dominant. He claims that, partly because of its vocational context, progressive education has been transformed into a form of conservative education. In that argument, what has taken place is a powerful subversion of progressive education, where student-centred learning can be viewed as a form of false consciousness. According to this argument, student-centred learning rarely involves real sharing of control but, by focusing on the individual learner, directs attention away from societal and institutional forms of 'disempowerment', for example due to inequalities of class, ethnicity or gender. In particular, there is an unquestioning acceptance of the social, political and economic status quo and an excessive emphasis on individualism that results in blaming the individual victims for their educational failures. This argument could be developed in relation to our earlier discussion of innovation in low status areas, the suggestion being that such a form of false consciousness is all the more important to foster amongst those who are most disadvantaged within society.

Arguments such as those advanced by Avis can lead us into a fatalistic or negative position, but they must be recognised and not ignored. Hodkinson (1994), in making the case for a more holistic model of empowerment addressing both the individualistic and communal forms, opens up more possibilities for us as teachers and educationists. Part of his argument is that progressive pedagogy is not automatically empowering. Rather, such approaches need to be adopted within a broader set of principles, including, for example, a commitment to the development of the ability to examine critically the contexts in which we live and learn.

A more recent student-centred development, within the broad vocational imperative, involves the student as consumer in a market environment. There are implications here for teaching and learning styles associated with the emphasis on flexible styles of delivery according to student need or demand. In addition, moves towards modularity, accreditation of prior experience and learning and student entitlement can be viewed as appreciative of consumer power, as can certain strands within the competency movement. A language has grown up here of students negotiating 'best deals' with, and within, educational institutions and training agencies of one form or another. Another way of putting it is that there is a shift to learner-centrism at the supposed cost of institutional power and this might, for some of us, be an important part of our own appreciation of student autonomy. We see this, for example, in the emerging language of post-16 institutions' and universities' mission statements.

At this point, it is important to distinguish between two rather different senses of student autonomy within the educational system. On the one hand there are matters to do with autonomy, empowerment and student-centredness within the actual teaching and learning process: for example to do with relationships between teacher and students within the classroom, to do with parameters for choice, say, as to the next activity for a student within a lesson, or relating to a piece of project work. On the other hand there are matters to do with autonomy, choice and responsibility for ones' own learning which are to do with charting a route into, through and out of an educational institution. Examples of the latter would be the extent to which, and the ways in which, students are allocated degrees of control and choice within modular programmes, in access to institutional resources and support structures or within overall course assessment patterns.

However, there are empirical questions regarding the ways in which, if at all, students as consumers and members of the 'real world' do in fact feel empowered in their negotiations with institutions. In the context of youth training, recent work by Hodkinson and Sparkes (1994) suggests that individual choices by young people were largely mythical and that other players, perhaps especially employers and training providers, had much more power to influence decisions about the nature of training. We need to know whether choices within schools, FE colleges or universities are similarly illusory or not. Certainly, evidence concerning the constraints placed on choice of university modules through demands for the study of prerequisite modules and through faculty ringfencing of students in the context of devolved cost centres leaves serious room for doubt that markets empower students at all (e.g. Hustler *et al.*, 1994b).

ADVANCING STUDENT-CENTRED LEARNING

Perhaps the one certainty about educational ideas is that there can be no consensus. In the recent past, student-centred learning and progressive education have been issues which tend to polarise both practitioners and thinkers. It is very easy to find eulogistic and almost messianic enthusiasms from protagonists, with varying degrees of sophistication. From such people, there is a sense that student-centred learning is a panacea for all ills, if only the rest of the world would realise it and join in. On the other hand, opponents see it as the root cause of almost all educational and social ills. Thus, for many in Britain, progressivism has become a term of abuse. There remains a deep suspicion within the classical humanist right wing, that a 'return' to didactic teaching of pupils sat silently in rows, combined with 'rigorous' pencil and paper tests, would lift British educational achievement to the levels of many of our economic rivals.

There is still too little accessible writing about these issues that avoids both extremes. In this chapter, we have tried to set out some of the issues more clearly, whilst trying to avoid such over-simplified hype. We began by pointing out the existence of a broad-based but loosely knit coalition in favour of student-centred approaches, and our arguments are primarily directed at those who can associate themselves with that coalition. For such people there may be some consensus, in general terms, regarding the relevance of the above arguments. They might also agree that student-centred learning practices are not exactly prevalent within schools, colleges and universities. There is some evidence that school developments in this area fostered through TVEI now have declining visibility, although we have yet to see where the post-Dearing adaptations to the National Curriculum will lead. It is also clear that student-centred learning is still only on the margins of the HE agenda, and here most commonly in vocational courses and in the lower status, ex-polytechnic universities (Brown and Scase, 1994). What, then, might foster a stronger, more general commitment to student-centred learning? This would presumably provide a necessary basis for continuity of student experience with regard to teaching and learning practices. There remains, however, a question as to the meaning of 'continuity' in this context. A brief discussion of these two questions concludes this chapter.

We would suggest that it is imperative to be much more explicit concerning the arguments supportive of student-centred learning: arguments perhaps such as those above, though they clearly need developing. Though these arguments do interrelate, there are recognisable differences between them, and certain arguments rather than others may be the really important ones for this or that group or institution. In brief, have those who, like us, are advocates of student-centred learning been clear enough about the grounds for our commitments? It is these grounds which presumably need to be both incorporated in institutional policy and drive staff development, as well as be made explicit to and with students. Any notion of student-centred learning must involve students in having access to the core arguments informing particular constellations of teaching and learning methodologies as well, perhaps, as access to the arguments behind certain forms of institutional provision more generally. This is, in our view, somewhat distinct from issues concerning the need for students to be aware of the criteria and aims of particular courses or programmes they embark on. 'Having access to' is one thing; recognising the validity of these arguments is something else. This then leads back to being prepared to, and having the capacity to, respond to challenges from staff or students regarding, for example, evidence or the underlying principles.

We would go further, and argue that advocates of student-centred learning need to become much more aware of the social and political context in which their work takes place. Those, like us, who believe education should do what it can to address the deep-seated inequalities of Western societies, need to recognise the dangers of an over-individualisation of 'responsibility', perhaps especially in a market context. As Ward and Mullender (1991) argue, disadvantaged groups may need to work collaboratively to improve their prospects, and education can help promote such radical ends. At the very least, we must avoid the dangers of an unintentional acceptance of a romanticised status quo, where conflicts can all be resolved by 'being reasonable' and inequalities are the result of merit and hard work alone.

The second question relates to how we might recognise 'student-centred learning' when we see it, and this has implications for coherence of institutional approaches and, therefore, consequences for continuity of student experience. Along with Entwistle, we are not suggesting that 'student-centred learning' is necessarily associated with the absence or presence of particular teaching and learning methods (nor for example, with this or that form of modular provision). The notion of continuity to be applied here is not based on the view that, for example, students should experience the same sort of open learning environment wherever they go, or that certain methods (e.g. didactic lectures) are intrinsically antithetical to learner autonomy. The point here is to do with the need to view any mix of teaching and learning methodologies (which students may experience) as explicitly informed by principles associated with learner autonomy and the underpinning commitments and arguments. The implication here is that the use of any particular method or methods in particular ways can be argued for and can be understood in relation to those principles. Here lies the basis for our recognition of 'student-centred learning' practices.

This returns us to the general drift of this chapter: in focusing on why we might wish to involve students more centrally, as more than the recipients of our wisdom, we need to explicate the supportive arguments. In doing this we are in a sense addressing desired learning outcomes for students in relation to certain pedagogical commitments. We also need to be ready to provide grounds, on occasion related to evidence and discussion as to what we might mean by evidence, concerning those arguments. However, this last point needs approaching with some caution. Accepting the virtues of public accountability does not always necessitate a search for, or a battle about, 'evidence' in the conventional sense. Presumably, there are certain arguments associated with how educational institutions should relate to students which do not stand or fall in relation to evidence. These may include matters of ethics for example. Once again, then, we return to the importance of being clear about the particular commitment arguments we are marshalling. Our concern in this chapter has been, in a very small-scale way, to attempt to start this process, at least for ourselves, in relation to commitments to 'student autonomy' and more specifically to 'students taking more control of their own learning'.

9

Higher Education – A Clear Sense of Vision?

Rob Halsall and David Hustler

INTRODUCTION

> The question of phased entry and accelerated degrees and differential output points, connects completely with the importance of understanding what someone actually did…increasing numbers and pressures mean we will have to…find ways of motivating students to learn how to learn, for their degree and for their life-long learning. This involves placing more responsibility upon the student…and differing responsibilities upon the institution. The Record of Achievement here is a device for making challenges explicit and tracking how you resolve them… this is also a device for avoiding replicating old learning experiences.
>
> (Vice Chancellor, old university)

> Recording achievement does seem to speak, in a variety of ways, to what we feel our purpose as a university is – our mission statement captures this. It also brings us into meaningful discussions with the institutions working with students before we do, certainly within the region. The RoA project and other associated projects link, in my view, with our commitment to mass higher education and to a changing notion of the typical university student.
>
> (Vice Chancellor, new university)

The two interview extracts above, whilst focusing on the relevance of the recording of achievement in the higher education context, point quite sharply to some of the issues to be discussed in this chapter. These statements, one coming from the Vice-Chancellor of a new university and the other from a Vice-Chancellor of an old university, point to not only a number of the forces for change operating in higher education (HE) but also suggest some ways in which senior personnel are responding, or planning to respond, to those forces. There are some distinct parallels here with many of the issues discussed in earlier chapters and associated developments in pre-university educational institutions. In this chapter we intend, first of all, to outline briefly some of these forces for change operating in HE, then move into some particular examples of developments in higher education institutions (HEIs) which relate to these forces, at least in part. We will then touch on some of the barriers to change in higher education.

Before doing this it is worth remembering that HE has traditionally been regarded as a powerful and somewhat independent shaper of much that has gone on in the secondary schooling sector, largely through control over entry and associated relationships with curriculum provision and assessment (in particular regarding O/GCSE and A-levels). That independence, we would argue, has diminished sharply over the last few years as HE has itself been subject to many of the forces for change which have had, and are having, an impact on other educational institutions. In general terms, the reference above to mission statements is interesting in itself, because it is clear that most universities are going through a process of establishing much more clearly what their particular priorities are and this, of course, has everything to do with the market in which they are operating and the associated sources of funding. Looking down the road a number of years we can anticipate a wider diversity of types of HEIs, in terms of the sort of student they are primarily aiming at, the relevance or otherwise of research to the institutions, the patterning and structuring of their degrees and the weighting between part-time and full-time degree routes and the extent to which they do or do not develop close links with pre-higher education institutions in their region.

FORCES FOR CHANGE

The authors of this chapter have, over the last 4 years, been involved in national evaluation work associated with the Employment Department, focusing on how a variety of universities, old and new, large and small, have been responding to initiatives in areas such as RoA and Guidance and Learner Autonomy. Part of this evaluation work has been concerned with the perceptions of university staff at different levels of responsibility and with a range of roles and professional concerns, regarding the current and future directions in which their own institution is travelling. The following overview of forces for change is derived from that evaluation work. In summary form the forces for change regarding HE are perceived to include at least the following:

- increasing and widening participation, together with the emerging debate on non-traditional entry routes and NCVQ developments;
- the quality assessment agenda;
- the employer perspective and the 'world of work';
- the developing focus on the student learning experience and the nature of learning outcomes;
- the diminution of resources, increasing student numbers and the need to find ways of students taking more responsibility for their own learning;
- the life-long learning agenda;
- the moves to modularity;
- the vocabularies of student empowerment, student choice, as well as consumerism and the charter movement;
- the revising of university missions and the juggling for university identity and relative position;
- the loosening of boundaries between HE and post-16 institutions;
- the changing views concerning what might count as an appropriate HE learning environment;
- the interest in obtaining funding relating to teaching and learning within HE.

This is an extensive list. Singling out a few of the themes, it seems appropriate to start with what some view as a shift towards a learning culture. A substantial proportion of existing provision in HE has traditionally been based on the notion that the most significant contribution to learning is made by teaching. One outcome of this has been the promotion of passive learning. However, it is increasingly recognised that knowledge does not exist independently of those who possess it, but fits into an existing framework of understanding and is shaped by that framework. The process of learning is an active one, students learning from their experiences through reflecting on them and through making sense of these reflections (Kolb, 1983). Increasingly, then, educationists are arguing that, 'There is an urgent need for all programmes of higher education...to be geared...to developing the skills of autonomous learning... the new emphasis in higher education must be on the process of learning' (Knowles, 1981:8).

The movement towards a more learner-centred approach is accompanied by a focus on what students are able to do, including what knowledge they have and what skills have been developed. This contrasts markedly with curriculum design being dominated by course intentions – the aims and objectives model – and goes some way towards explaining the growing emphasis on competences and learning outcomes, and a shift towards criterion-referenced assessment. There has been, of course, a long history of competence and outcomes-based provision but it has been somewhat peripheral. As a 'total system' the emphasis stems from the New Training Initiative (started in 1981) with its introduction of the concept of standards, leading eventually to NVQ criteria, the establishment of National Training and Education Targets and the emergence of NVQ and GNVQ awards. The debate surrounding competences and learning outcomes – their purposes, shades of meaning, how best to harmonise them – is not resolved as yet, but it has highlighted a key question: 'What have graduates learned and what can they "do"?' For too long, it is argued, this has gone unasked, but the 'accountable curriculum' expected in a period of international competitiveness and tight resources presses ever more on HE. Without doubt, the work on learning outcomes undertaken by UDACE (Otter, 1992) will be built-upon increasingly in curriculum design, and developments within the NCVQ framework will probably spread within HE sooner rather than later.

There are related developments associated with the student becoming more at the centre of attention, developments linked with modularity and the language of student empowerment and student choice. The very fact of providing students with opportunities within a course to take an active role in shaping how they learn, what they learn and/or where they learn itself represents empowerment of students. Increasingly, however, students are also able, within defined parameters, to construct their own course. This results from the trend towards modularity which has occurred for one or more reasons, some 'educational' and others more pragmatic, but all with the same effect of providing greater choice. Thus, some institutions have introduced modularity so as to enable students to take a more broadly-based education; to delay their final choice of route; to enter and exit at different points of the year or of their lives; to mix on- and off-site learning. At the same time, it has not gone unnoticed that modularisation can provide a boost to recruitment: through offering students more choice of unit combinations, institutions can advertise a seemingly infinite number of courses and named awards. It can also, of course, provide economies of scale with modules being shared rather than duplicated across different departments or courses. There are also two other forces working towards student choice and empowerment. First, although the Charter for Higher Education is somewhat controversial, it does signal a clear commitment to the notion of student rights and it will raise student awareness that HE providers are accountable for what they claim will be delivered. Second, additional tuition fees for full-time courses is on the agenda. This will surely enhance the notion of students as consumers, and HEIs as suppliers will ignore student needs, demands, and expectations at their own risk.

The pressure towards more accountability to the students as consumers is interrelated with pressure from employers. Concern has been expressed by employers and government that HEIs give insufficient attention to the relevance of their curricula to the world of work. In particular, it is claimed that skills required in everyday work situations are not being developed sufficiently. Most often cited are skills relating to communication, problem-solving, self-reliability, collaboration, and critical evaluation. As expressed by Robertson (1992:23), 'The pulse of modern society is out of harmony with the indulgent progress of learning that has characterised undergraduate careers to date'. Consequently, the government has pursued a strategy to re-orientate education and training in the light of its views as to how schools, colleges and now also universities can better meet the perceived needs of industry and, in addition, to widen access to this education and training. The issue of widening access brings us to increasing and widening participation in HE. The sector is rapidly expanding despite the recent moratorium. By the year 2000 there will be more than one million undergraduates, and an increasing proportion of these will be people in employment or with previous work experience and people from groups traditionally under-represented in HE. Moreover, an increasing proportion of the 18–19-year old-entrants will be drawn from non-A-level routes, not least GNVQ. Access will no longer be a marginal activity; HE will be seen more as an entitlement. The initial push for expansion has itself stimulated demand, presaging the imminence of a virtuous circle of aspiration and achievement (Ball, 1990).

The expansion of HE raises questions about the nature and purpose of the sector because it challenges existing structures and cultures. Thus the needs of adult students to learn at times and in places of their own convenience must be recognised. At the same time it will be necessary to look closely at the sorts of experiences 18–19-year-old entrants have had, not just within GNVQ programmes but also in the A-level context which is already being reshaped partly as a result of the emergence of GNVQs. More generally, the exploration of alternative learning environments and experiences might well be a necessary response to the increasing pressure on University space and tutor's time, apart from being a desirable response to the recognition that much valuable learning can, and does, take place outside of lecture halls and seminar rooms (a factor already acted upon by many course teams in their operation of assessment of prior experiential learning).

Crucially, and to return to Ball's paper, it is argued that more cannot mean more of the same: it has to mean something different. But how can the system be adapted to meet the challenge without a deterioration in what is already delivered? Indeed, how can we have more and better? This question is brought into sharp relief by quality assessment within HE. The assessment of course design and the quality of teaching and learning have become important items on the HE agenda, as has the auditing of systems for ensuring the quality of provision. Indeed, funding councils use quality assessments as one factor in the funding model for teaching in HEIs. Assessors' judgements are based on their assessment of the quality of student achievement, the student learning experience and the effectiveness of teaching/learning and assessment methods and whether the student experience is enhanced through effective academic and personal support. Increasingly, criteria being applied in coming to such judgements include those to do with students' understanding of course aims and objectives, their active involvement in learning and whether they leave with transferable knowledge and skills.

Finally, the nature of the student experience is increasingly being put in the context of life-long learning. HEIs do not exist in a vacuum. Life goes on both before and after the student's HE experience. This has already been alluded to in discussion of the employer perspective, the growing number of mature students and changes in pre-HE education, not least the introduction of GNVQs with its outcomes-led approach and emphasis on core skills, a shifting of A-levels towards GNVQ and the development of a modular post-16 framework which will facilitate shared units across GNVQ and A-level studies. Moreover, there are structural changes. Reference has been made to the integration of work-based degree programmes. There is also, of course, the development of HE/FE partnerships in such forms as franchised courses, 2 + 2 degrees and associate college arrangements. In short, the attitudes and structures are in place for the 'take-off' of 'lifelong learning'. Post-16 education is expanding and merging with HE. Employers recognise the need for high-level education and training. Additionally, there is increasingly a substantial 'senior citizenship', including many early retirees used to education and training, who will be looking for enrichment. Higher education, then, is a stage in a learning career, not a final learning experience. HEIs need to take note of this fact and its implications, not least for issues of coherence, continuity and progression in the student learning experience.

DEVELOPMENTS IN HIGHER EDUCATION

Given the nature of several of the forces acting on HE identified above it is not surprising that the Employment Department (ED), with its concerns for skills enhancement, vocational qualifications, lifelong learning and the development of flexible and adaptable learners and workers, emerged as a key player in teaching and learning developments in HE. Its first major incursion came with the Enterprise in Higher Education (EHE) initiative which is now in its seventh year and involves over 20,000 employers and 250,000 students to a greater or lesser extent in a variety of initiatives (see, e.g. Darkes and Silvester, 1994; Heywood, 1994; University of Portsmouth, 1993). Subsequently, the ED has prioritised a more narrowly focused body of research and development projects including those supported through its Higher Education Projects Funds (HEPF). Here, we focus on illustrative developments drawing principally, though not solely, on initiatives with which we have been involved in an external evaluation capacity: the Recording Achievement and Higher Education (ROAHE) Project, which was part-funded by the ED, and the ED's 1994–95 HEPF Themes.

Recording achievement and higher education

Certainly, recording achievement is on the HE agenda. The work of Fenwick *et al.* (1992) was the major published outcome of an ED-funded project on work-based learning in academic courses and a CNAA-funded project on recording student achievements in CNAA courses. These two projects involved 24 case studies of profiling or recording achievement systems, whilst Assiter and Shaw's book (1993) includes a further nine HE case studies. However, our focus is the ROAHE Project. This initially involved 15 HEIs and 11 LEAs and associated schools and colleges in the north of England. Its aims included that of encouraging HEIs to use recording achievement as a formative process to improve the quality and effectiveness of learning. Our evaluation identified three outcomes of Project activity in relation to this aim (Hustler *et al.*, 1994a:50):

> It has resulted in an interest at HE level which is concerned with recording achievement as a developmental process which encourages more reflective students who are able to assess achievements and action plan....It has encouraged HE departments/faculties/courses to consider ways in which current course activities can be enhanced by the adoption or extension of RoA processes....It has provided opportunities for the development of new course initiatives...which acknowledge the use of RoA processes as valuable in improving the quality and effectiveness of learning.

Many of these course developments illustrate work in the areas of personal skills profiling, core skills tracking or professional work-based reviewing which focus on the use of recording achievement skills in varied contexts. Case studies have been provided by the Project (ROAHE Project, 1994). For instance, the Department of Biomedical Sciences at the University of Bradford emphasises personal and academic profiling as an opportunity for self-identification of strengths and limitations in respect of particular skills and concepts relevant to vocational aspirations and for enabling the setting of realistic curriculum targets. In the Department of German at the University of Leeds two related schemes were introduced. One is based on the keeping of a log by students undertaking their year abroad to help them articulate their learning from that experience. The other developed out of that scheme and involves the use of a personal skills portfolio throughout the degree.

In UMIST's Department of Computation the recording achievement initiative is closely linked to the British Computer Society's Professional Development Scheme. Its aims are to facilitate the personal and professional development of students, to provide them with a mechanism for planning and monitoring that development, to assist them in their preparation for careers and to improve their ability to present themselves advantageously to employers. A *Professional Development Manual* allows for each student to undertake action planning based on academic achievement, professional development and career strategy. Its main purpose, in fact, is to help ease entry into the workforce.

As a final example from the case studies, at the University of Huddersfield a wide range of courses are utilising one form or another of recording achievement. For example, in history and politics the focus is on learning from a work placement while in textiles and social work courses the concern is for the development of 'enterprise' and transferable personal skills throughout the programmes. These are also the focus in hotel and catering business but a feature here has been a specific personal and transferable skills module with its *Professional Development Journal* which includes a self-administered skills audit and a student learning contract to facilitate a plan of action.

What we wish to draw out from these ROAHE Project case studies, and the same applies to others provided by Fenwick and Assiter and Shaw, is the particular emphasis on the issue of employability and the relationship of personal and other 'transferable' skills to this. Certainly, there is a prevalence of vocationally-oriented courses or workplace components of other courses, across the case studies. Here, McCulloch's point (1993:57) is pertinent: 'It's probably no accident that most of the development in RoA processes in HE has been in those courses which most approximate to the work situation itself'.

Higher Education Projects Fund (HEPF)

In order to build on such projects as the ROAHE and EHE, the ED introduced its HEPF in 1993 and it is to this that we now turn. The Fund invited project proposals related to three themes. These were Guidance and Learner Autonomy (GLA), Work-based Learning (WBL) and Credit Frameworks and Learning Outcomes (CFLO). Over 160 bids were received, mainly from HEIs as single institutions or in partnership with other institutions including other HEIs and Training and Enterprise Councils. Twenty projects were selected, work to be undertaken over 1994–95.

The six projects within the GLA theme aim to 'produce a coherent institutional policy and implementation strategy, for an area of work which is often haphazard and uncoordinated' (DoE, 1994:2). Within this overall concern the projects are variously focusing on specific developments:

- educational guidance at different stages of students' lives: pre-entry, at induction and during the programme of study;
- careers education and guidance through careers modules, careers education materials and the development of departmental careers tutors' networks;
- personal tutoring systems, sometimes in tandem with self-assessment, profiling and recording achievement initiatives;
- researching the nature of learner autonomy and student characteristics;
- defining more clearly the roles of central support services and developing the relationships between internal and external guidance systems.

The seven WBL projects 'focus on ways in which people at work can gain HE and Vocational Qualifications using their work experience as evidence of learning' (DoE, 1994:7). They follow in the wake of several previous ED-funded WBL initiatives, the key concerns being to develop more flexible assessment systems and modes of working which provide the rigour sought by HE while being of benefit to employers and employees. The projects variously include:

- developing academic units which incorporate occupational standards and integrating NVQ units into mainstream academic awards;
- developing the possibility for full university qualifications to be gained through wholly work-based learning;
- encouraging university students to acquire NVQs during work placements;
- extending existing access to HE by work-based learning to local colleges of further education;
- developing and delivering an access programme provided in small

to medium-sized enterprises;

- establishing a network of employers with a view to identifying and supporting the links between employer training and HE activity;
- improving performance in industrial sectors which are dependent on advanced research and development by providing links between university research centres and industrial partners.

Whereas much of the WBL activity is about the equivalence of university and work-based learning, the CFLO Theme is to do with 'Creating greater harmony between academic qualifications' (DoE, 1994:12). The seven projects are concerned with identifying equivalence between the university and the vocational qualifications credit systems and enabling people to make progress using whichever system is appropriate to their needs. Activities across the projects include:

- developing a model for the interpretation of Advanced GNVQ programmes into HEI award routes and thence making recommendations on its application in a national credit framework;
- informing the development of NVQs and GNVQs at level 4 and beyond;
- extending and developing an existing access course to degree level in the context of a credit framework which recognises NVQs and GNVQs at pre-degree and degree levels;
- integrating NVQ and GNVQ units into existing academic structures and developing equivalences between these units and academic credits;
- producing an open learning resource pack which will enable HE staff to design programmes and modules which will emphasise competence-based learning, include a generic core curriculum and enable the use of this to enhance the coherence of modular programmes of study.

Across these three themes and within the ROAHE case studies, then, we can detect a number of manifestations of some of the forces we pointed to earlier as acting upon HE. Thus, we note the concerns for improving and extending careers education, developing transferable core skills, developing more autonomous learners and ensuring the status both of vocational qualifications and work-based learning through determining their equivalence with academic awards and university-based study (at times by the use of competence frameworks). In turn these are, of course, redolent of the issues focused on in this book in relation to the 14–19 sector. A key issue, however, is to what extent will such initiatives become rooted in HE? We have noted earlier the forces for change but what are the barriers?

BARRIERS TO CHANGE

What sorts of forces are there that might make it difficult for some of the developments explored in the preceding section to take a firm and pervasive hold in HE? In attempting to answer this question, we draw on our early evaluation of the GLA theme (Hustler *et al.*, 1994b). We are not suggesting that all of our findings necessarily apply, either at all or equally, to all initiatives. Moreover, we recognise that they relate to GLA activity in its early stages and that projects might well surmount the difficulties we identify. Nevertheless, we do believe that they represent at least some of the barriers to lasting change in HE and that those involved in different developments will recognise some of them. Essentially they are to do with finance, human resources, institutional cultures, change strategies and conceptual understanding.

Although many people in the HE sector will admit that significant change and progress can be made with limited, additional funding, the fact of the matter is that in recent years there has been an actual squeeze in the funding of the HE sector. In particular, the income per student has decreased and student–staff ratios have risen. In this climate it could be difficult for either senior management or 'grassroots staff' to prioritise the sort of developmental work described in the preceding section. Thus, from senior managers of project institutions:

> The financial squeeze is eroding the educational experience...if this squeeze from government continues then very good things like these projects may get squeezed out. It does need resourcing....The Executive wants to be as supportive as possible towards the project, but has to balance that support in principle when it comes to prioritising conflicting resource demands. (Hustler *et al.*, 1994b:7)

More, and often conflicting, demands are also being experienced by the majority of academic staff. The 'research imperative' has always been important in the old universities where:

The Project coincides with the last spurt of activity on the next research rating round and colleagues will be under considerable pressure to publish quickly. This will produce job tensions for many…there is still a predominantly research focus; teaching developments are relatively low status…beginning to change but there's a long way to go. (Hustler *et al.* 1994b, p.7)

Indeed, the pressure to publish is increasingly felt by the new universities and by Colleges of Higher Education too. However, the research thrust is just one dimension and senior managers themselves are expressing anxiety on behalf of their staff concerning overload. As succinctly put by one Vice-Chancellor, 'I have an overwhelming impression of staff struggling to keep their heads above water…the project won't have been high on the agenda in some cases…the major barrier is sheer staff exhaustion' (Hustler *et al.*, 1994b:8). Certainly, there does come across from our interviews in particular – many of which were with senior managers and staff heavily involved in project management – that in their view, many of the academic staff located in departments are not yet especially committed to the projects and/or their concerns. A key question here must be whether these attitudes – if these views are indeed an accurate reflection of such – are due to 'exhaustion' rather than to a negative stance as regards project concerns. Certainly, given that achievement of the long-term aims of projects, especially that of taking root across the sector generally, depends upon involvement and commitment by a high proportion of staff, there could be some cause for concern regarding their success though we repeat that the evaluation work we are drawing on was at an early stage of project life.

This situation could be seen to be exacerbated by the nature and management of HEIs. First, it is difficult in practical terms to talk about the staff of an institution. This, in a sense, presumes that we can envisage the institution as a homogeneous entity. Usually this is far from being the case. Staff cover numerous subject areas which are often located on different sites. Moreover, departments – and sometimes whole faculties or schools – often have their own histories and traditions which go back beyond the existence of the institution as it is today. A typical 'new' university has been formed out of a succession of mergers: the Mechanics Institute, the College of Art and Design, the School of Hotel and Catering, one or more teacher-training colleges, and so on. There are, beyond the level of the individual member of staff, different concerns and thrusts; sandwich and vocational courses here, the 'caring' professions there, the 'commercial' professions in that corner, liberal education in the other. Some have always had a major concern for issues related to student learning and some have always been strong on guidance matters but not all have by any means. Juxtapose this historical diversity of cultures and traditions with an overarching culture of individual staff autonomy, a strongly devolved and largely departmental management structure and a general lack of centralisation as regards what students actually experience in 'the classroom' and it is not surprising that there is rarely to be found in HEIs any co-ordinated, shared approach to teaching and learning initiatives.

There are resource issues here too. HEIs have been keen to devolve budgetary management to internal cost centres, so decisions about how to spend money and commit staff are being taken ever more separately within institutions. Such budgetary management is not conducive to central thrusts or co-ordinated approaches. Indeed, it can be directly at odds with particular concerns. In relation to student choice, for example, because cost-centres usually reflect subject boundaries there is a tendency to ring-fence their income sources, the students. The effect can be to reconsolidate the traditional unilinear course even within an allegedly high-choice modular system. As Robertson (1994) points out, if devolved budgetary management is to be made consonant with student choice – and to this we might well add student guidance – it may be necessary to consider the separation of devolved budgetary management from the management of student programmes. Indeed, some commentators have suggested that it might be necessary to consider the direct empowerment of students by financial entitlement.

The adoption of the most appropriate change strategies is another central issue and directly relates to the 'style' of institutional management and institutional culture. There is no doubt that project managers are faced with searching questions regarding more and less likely successful change strategies. Certainly, tensions abound:

> There's an acceptance of the need to change but the process can exacerbate old tensions, for example between the centre and departments as to who does what and provides what. The project can be caught up in that tension. (Hustler *et al.*, 1994b:12)

In one sense, many project managers are faced with a dilemma. They often have senior management support but this can be tempered by a reluctance or inability to impose change on staff. At the same time many staff are reluctant, for whatever reason, to commit themselves to project concerns. Where more centralised strategies are adopted they can be pursued unevenly and in any case might gain the involvement, but not win the hearts and commitment, of staff. Where more devolutionist strategies are employed these too can lead to uneven involvement and, indeed, might result in helping to perpetuate the kinds of uncoordinated and piecemeal activities that have previously occurred.

Finally, we raise as a possible barrier to lasting and pervasive change the issue of shared understanding of the nature and purpose of the intended change. Many writers have commented on the necessity of a shared vision for successful innovation (e.g. Fullan, 1991). However, in the early interview data we collected on the learner autonomy focus within the GLA theme, it was apparent that there are wide variations in the ways in which this is conceptualised. As one participant said, 'meanings in this area are a source for confusion. We can easily talk at cross purposes.' These variations can be important for the ultimate success of the theme as a whole and the individual projects within it. This is because the conceptual perceptions of project participants will have a major impact on their practice, differing but unexplored conceptions between participants may lead to tensions and conflicts between them and it is possible that hidden within conceptual confusions lie incompatible objectives and/or activities which are at odds with each other, rather than working in harmony.

To illustrate with reference to learner autonomy, some participants expressed clear views of a coherent schema that governed their intentions and actions. Others, however, were much less clear about the central meaning of the notion and even where perceptions were clear, they took different forms for different individuals. Views about what autonomy actually means fell along a spectrum between two different models. For some, autonomy focused on self-regulated learning, whilst for others autonomy was seen as being about making decisions and choices. Thus:

For me it's about students taking responsibility for their own learning: learning from each other, learning to learn. Students [should be] able to operate in ways which free them from some at least of their current, considerable dependence on staff (and)....The intention is that the project will enable the development of systems re teaching and learning and guidance, which encourage independence, autonomy and enable students to make choices and decisions related to their learning, e.g. related to employment choices and careers. (Hustler *et al.*, 1994b:21)

CONCLUDING COMMENTS

The title of the Society for Research in Higher Education 1995 National Conference – 'The Changing University' – is indicative of some of the themes we have addressed in this chapter and elsewhere in this book. However, and not least in the light of the preceding section, we would not want to exaggerate the extent to which HE is changing. There is little doubt that for a considerable number of students the nature of their university experience is very different from what it would have been 10 years ago. However, the extent of change has been distinctly uneven both within and across institutions. This has led to increasing diversity in the nature of the student experience. It is our view that diversity within a university is likely over the next 10 years to be much less important than that between them. Currently universities are, as noted earlier, going through a process of trying to establish what sort of institutions they are, who their central clients are, what market or market-niche they should aim for, whether or not they can take themselves seriously as centres of research, what precisely their mission is (or has to be!). The signs are already clear, for example, that for many universities their student market will be local or regional whereas others will maintain or build a national profile. Certain universities will rely more on their research funding than their 'teaching' funding and many universities will drop research aspirations off their agenda altogether.

In brief, we envisage a clearer mix of different types of university, with associated differences in terms of the sort of student they attract, the sort of admission requirements they impose and the nature of the student experience they provide. Very possibly, only some of these will view as a priority the sorts of developments outlined earlier. A picture which currently seems more 'chaotic' than 'coherent' is likely to become more coherent, at least in terms of higher education systems' predictability. One might argue that this form of coherence is to be welcomed, though some might note uneasy parallels with the Secondary Modern, Technical and Grammar post-1944 schooling variants and that too was welcomed initially as a 'coherent' system! If this prediction were to prove accurate, the key issue in relation to the theme of this book is whether a backwash effect might occur that would reinforce the divisiveness that is to be found currently in 14–19 education and training. In short, such a trend could continue, or re-kindle, HE's role as a powerful shaper of what goes on in the secondary and FE sectors.

10

Chaos or Coherence, Progression and Continuity

Mike Cockett

A story is told of a young boy who was having difficulty learning to read. He struggled for a long time and then the light dawned. 'Oh it's the black bits you have to look at,' he said, 'not the white bits.' Of course he was right, but on mature reflection he will probably realise that, though it is true that the letters and words are printed in black in most books, they depend for their existence on the white bits, the spaces in between. This book has concentrated on the spaces in between, focusing not on the content of the curriculum nor, on the whole, on effective ways of teaching that curriculum, but on issues of assessment, of transfer of information and of progression. The focus has been on the results of a range of initiatives and projects aimed at those issues. Key questions have been asked about how best to recognise the results of teaching and learning programmes, how best to manage learning, how best to transfer information about achievement and how best to give all young people a sense of making progress and of becoming qualified. The rhetoric behind some of the developments examined has been beguilingly attractive. It is easy to agree that:

- what is significant about a teaching and learning programme is what is learnt rather than what is taught;
- the results of training should be greater competence in the work place;
- having learnt one body of knowledge or one set of skills then some core knowledge or skill can be transferred to new areas of learning;
- the quality of a person is represented better by a rounded record of achievement than by a set of examination grades;
- some pupils are better able to cope with a practical curriculum than an academic one;

- standards can only be raised by expecting more of students and setting them, and their teachers, clear achievement goals.

Each of the chapters in the book has been an examination of what happens when attempts are made to put this sort of rhetoric into practice. We see, for example, in Hodkinson's chapter on National Vocational Qualifications (Chapter 3), that descriptions of competence and work-based assessment run the risk of further ossifying outdated practices. Records of Achievement, as Halsall illustrates (Chapter 7), have been widely developed but the claims of the pioneers that they would enhance learning and lead to a more effective transfer of information have yet to be justified and Cockett and Callaghan (Chapter 5) illustrate the negative effects on many students of setting a high GCSE bench mark. The fact is that in each of these areas, major problems have emerged which illustrate how much we do not yet know.

It has become a commonplace to propose that we face a future in which change is endemic. What we have still to learn is how we move systems and institutions from stasis to engagement with the process of change. All educational establishments would claim that they are already having to change all the time but the question is raised, most clearly by Halsall and Hustler in their review of developments in higher education (Chapter 9), of whether apparent activity denotes fundamental change or whether the volume of competing demands coupled with a squeeze on resources encourages resistance. This may particularly apply when attempts are made to implement and disseminate the positive results of pilot programmes. At the other end of the academic scale, Cockett explores the mechanisms by which change is resisted (Chapter 4), not always in conscious rear-guard actions but through processes akin to tissue rejection, arising more from individual psychology than political or pedagogic commitment.

Overlying all this is the problem of predicting economic and educational futures. Not only is it difficult to gather enough information and expertise about what is going on now, we are in the position of all forecasters when faced with turbulent conditions of having to draw in our sights and be content with predicting that conditions will be changeable. We will never have enough information to predict with great accuracy either individual, group or society futures. For this reason, we have to live with a level of chaos. However, we should make a distinction here between the 'deterministic chaos' which we recognise as being the inevitable consequence of working and living in complex circumstances (Fullan, 1993) and a sort of 'culpable chaos' which arises from an inability or unwillingness to address the structural anomalies which we could do something about.

Hargreaves (1994) describes three common responses to the post-modern condition. The first is to hark back to some supposed golden age, the second is to attempt to impose order from the centre and the third is to back off completely and leave it all to forces recognisably out of control. Currently, political pressure is to respond in all three ways at the same time. The A-level 'gold standard' must be retained; team games in school will reinvigorate lost British virtues; a National Curriculum rigorously tested, National Vocational Qualifications and standardisation in everything from GCSE to higher degrees will bring clarity and confidence and, in the end, market forces will decide. The concerns expressed in this book are enough to make us wary of all three responses. In particular we should be wary of global solutions aimed at imposing coherence for the sake of simplicity and manageability without regard for unforeseen consequences. It may seem somewhat perverse, given the title of the book, to suggest that what we are looking for is neither chaos nor coherence. What is required is a coherent approach to living with chaos – flexible, responsive, learning structures and a dialogue between competing forces rather than attempts to back winners.

PROGRESSION AND CONTINUITY

It is the students in our schools, colleges and universities who are at the sharp end of all this. Cockett and Callaghan examine transition at 16+ (Chapter 5) and ask questions about the sort of deal we are offering young people. Reasonably, young people want their work to count in some way. They are disappointed and discouraged when it appears to come to nothing. The transition into post-compulsory education and training is only the first move into an adult world which promises a lifetime of uncertainties. It is easy to take the grand view and see that jobs for life are going to be the exception rather than the rule but it is the young people now entering that world who have to learn how to manage their lives in that context. The emphasis on work-related and career-related innovations funded by the Employment Department in higher education, discussed by Halsall and Hustler (Chapter 9), demonstrate that such uncertainties are expected to affect all levels of employment. The concern for learner autonomy, for student-centred learning, is seen by Hustler and Hodkinson (Chapter 8) to stem not only from the need to develop the most effective styles of teaching and learning but also from a need to promote flexibility and self-motivation in individual students.

One solution proposed to a number of these issues is that there should be an overarching structure of diplomas which will be available to all and which will combine academic and vocational traditions. Such diplomas will offer a continuity from one level to another and an equivalence of status between different courses at the same level. The notion has its attractions and at least offers an improvement on the current status ridden and badly understood mixture. But history and tradition cannot easily be set on one side. Halsall and Hustler (Chapter 9) question whether an emerging, more coherent but differentiated higher education will not simply be another manifestation of the tripartite system but at a higher level.

Similarly, users of any new diploma will wish to set it in a known context. Versions of it will be explained as being the same as five GCSEs or the same as three A-levels and before long the old divisions will emerge. The National Commission on Education (1993) in explaining its proposals for an advanced level General Education Diploma did so in terms of entry into higher education. Although the diploma is to be for all, they retain a distinction between those following the traditional academic route and those approaching the diploma through traineeships. Gleeson (Chapter 2) also proposes that an essential part of a 'new educational settlement' would be a unified national qualification system. On balance the evidence in this book would support that notion, but with reservations. At this stage we can do little more than say we must avoid the status trap into which those pursuing 'equivalence' and 'parity of esteem' will inevitably fall. The point is not to attack the Commission's proposal for a new diploma but to illustrate how difficult it is to move to something new without carrying forward problems which the reform is intended to overcome. As with coherence, continuity may prove ephemeral. Perhaps we will have to learn how to live with discontinuity.

On the other hand, it does seem pragmatically and philosophically right that all young people should be offered the means of making progress, if for no other reason than that the economic and social cost of not doing so will be unsupportable. The challenge is to develop

systems which allow each phase to build on the previous phase but which also provide for changes of direction and new possibilities. Students need to be surprised into finding out what they want to do with their lives as much as they need to be encouraged to plan a future. Halsall, in his discussion of Records of Achievement (Chapter 7), warns against systems which aim to be so tight that they invade privacy and reduce the rights and responsibilities of learners. What we need to develop is an overall framework with clear routes of progression for all abilities and which at the same time allows for the accidents, the surprises and the enforced changes of direction which, we are told, is the future for most young people. What we need to avoid is a system of cul-de-sacs involving constant retreat before redirection.

Progression can be seen both in terms of qualifications for all abilities and in terms of increasing command of the processes of learning. Hustler and Hodkinson touch on this second issue (Chapter 8). The rhetoric behind the notion of learner autonomy comes from two directions. The first is the belief that learner autonomy is the way towards more effective learning and the second comes from the prevailing sense that if the learner does not manage the learning then no one else will. On the other hand this individualism must be balanced against societal needs for economically productive individuals who are educated and trained to fit the required roles. This is another important dilemma which can be faced coherently. The need is for systems which address the issue of the balance between the individual needs to follow interests, to become financially independent and to retain a sense of self worth, with social, cultural and economic needs.

As this book goes to press Sir Ron Dearing has published his interim report on post-16 qualifications (Dearing, 1995). It contains a welcome recognition of many of the issues raised here. Along with the formation of the new Department for Education and Employment, there seems to be, at last, some recognition that there is a need for an overarching national framework. It is unfortunate that the review begins at 16. Many would argue, as we would, that an opportunity is being missed in not including qualifications at 16. There is recognition in the report that imagining a new framework is only part of the task ahead. Ensuring its acceptance could prove even more difficult. Here, we believe, the studies in this book become particularly relevant. If the framework is to have any chance of success then those designing

and implementing it must address the same issues of culture and vested interests and status and psychology which have beset all previous attempts to make radical changes. Perhaps the deepest problem of all will be to marry the two aspirations to retain the 'rigour of A-levels' and to provide for all levels of ability. A-levels carry with them all the cultural associations of selection and status and normative grading which for us almost define what is meant by ability. The shift required is a massive one, from the notion of ability as, more or less, a fixed quality of an individual to the notion of everyone becoming more able as they progress through life, albeit at their own pace. We are still struggling to accept that intelligence is not a fixed commodity.

All this reflects, and provides some detailed backing for, Gleeson's call for a new educational settlement (Chapter 2). If global economies and developments in technology make our local economic futures unpredictable then the same is true of our education and training futures. Simple rhetoric or simple theories prescribing solutions to our educational ills, however attractive, lead to unimagined complexities when the attempt is made to turn theories and rhetoric into action. For this, if for no other reason, the new educational settlement must be a partnership through which we recognise the legitimate concerns of many players, economists, politicians, managers, teachers, workers and students. The partnership would be a recognition that a solution to complex and constantly changing problems will not be found within and cannot be imposed by any particular sectional interest. Leading such a partnership will be much more like running an orchestra than running a supermarket. Success will depend on harnessing experience, skills, knowledge and expertise built up over many years from many different sources and traditions. We cannot be certain of the outcome but we can retain a vision that the whole will somehow be greater than a collection of individual parts.

References

Ashworth, P. D. and Saxton, J. (1990) 'On Competence', *Journal of Further and Higher Education*, **14(2)**, 1–25.

Assiter, A. and Shaw, E. (eds) (1993) *Using Records of Achievement in Higher Education*. London: Kogan Page.

Atkinson, J. W. (1957) 'Motivational Determinants of Risk Taking Behaviour', *Psychological Review*, **64**, 359–72.

Avis, J. (1991a) 'Curriculum Categories and Student Identities in FE', in *Education Limited*. Department of Cultural Studies, University of Birmingham. London: Unwin Hyman.

Avis, J. (1991b) 'The strange fate of progressive education', in *Education Group II, Education Limited: Schooling and Training and the New Right Since 1979*. London: Unwin Hyman.

Avis, J. (1992) 'Social Difference and Antagonism Within the 16–19 Core Curriculum', *British Journal of Sociology of Education*, **13(3)**, 361–373.

Baddeley, G. (1991) 'Teachers and Learners', in Hustler, D., Cockett, M. and Milroy, E. (eds) *Learning Environments for the Whole Curriculum*. London: Unwin Hyman.

Ball, C. (1990) *More Means Different: Widening Access to Higher Education*. London: RSA.

Ball, C., *et al.* (1991) *Learning Pays*. London: RSA.

Barnes, D. (1976) *From Communication to Curriculum*. Harmondsworth: Penguin.

Barnes, D. (1989) *Active Learning*. University of Leeds, TVEI Support Unit.

Barnett, R. (1994) *The Limits of Competence: Knowledge, Higher Education and Society*. Open University Press.

Barrow, R. (1987) 'Skill Talk', *Journal of Philosophy of Education*, **21(2)**, 187–99.

Berkeley, J. (1992) 'Promoting Lifelong Learning through Education Partnership', *Education and Training*, **34(2)**, 3–7.

Black, H. and Wolf, A. (1990) (eds) *Knowledge and Competence: Current issues in Training and Education*. London: COIC.

Bloomer, G., Lester, N., Onore, C. and Cook, J. (1992) (eds) *Negotiating the Curriculum: Educating for the 21st Century*. Lewes: Falmer.

Bloomer, M. and Morgan, D. (1993) 'It is Planned, Therefore it Happens – Or Does It?', *Journal of Further and Higher Education*, **17(1)**, 22–37.

Boud, D. (1981) *Developing Autonomy in Learning*. London: Kogan Page.

Brandes, D. and Ginnis, P. (1986) *A Guide to Student-Centred Learning*. Oxford: Blackwell.

Brause, R. S. (1992) *Enduring Schools: Problems and Possibilities*. Lewes: Falmer.

Bridges, D. (1993) 'Transferable Skills: A Philosophical Perspective'. *Studies in Higher Education*, **18(1)**, 43–51.

Broadfoot, P. (ed.) (1986) *Profiles and Records of Achievement: A Review of Issues and Practice*. London: Cassell.

Brown, A. and Evans, K. (1994) 'Changing the Training Culture: Lessons from Anglo-German Comparisons of Vocational Education and Training'. *British Journal of Education and Work*, **7(2)**, 5–16.

Brown, J. S., Collins, A. and Duguid, P. (1989) 'Situated Cognition and the Culture of Learning', *Educational Researcher*, **18(1)**, 32–42.

Brown, P. and Scase, R. (1994) *Higher Education and Corporate Realities: Class, Culture and the Decline of Graduate Careers*. London: UCL Press.

BTEC (1993a) *Implementing BTEC GNVQs: a Guide for Centres*. London: BTEC.

BTEC (1993b) *GNVQ Core Skills*. London: BTEC.

Burgess, R. G. (1988) 'Whatever happened to the Newsom Course?' in Pollard, A., Purvis, J. and Wallford, G. (eds) *Education, Training and the New Vocationalism*. Milton Keynes: Open University Press.

Burgess, T. and Adams, E. (1986) 'Records for all at 16' in Broadfoot, P. (ed.) *Profiles and Records of Achievement: A Review of Issues and Practice*. London: Cassell.

Burke, J. (1989) (ed.) *Competence Based Education and Training*. Lewes: Falmer.

Burke, J. (1995) (ed.) *Outcomes, Learning and the Curriculum: Implications for NVQs, GNVQs and Other Qualifications*. Lewes: Falmer.

CBI (1989) *Towards a Skills Revolution: Report of the Vocational Education and Training Task Force*. London: CBI.

CBI (1993) *Routes to Success*. London: CBI.

Coates, P. (1991) 'The 16–19 core skills initiative', *The Curriculum Journal*, **2(1)**, 43–53.

Cobb, P. (1994) 'Where is the Mind? Constructivist and Sociocultural Perspectives on Mathematical Development', *Educational Researcher*, **23(7)**, 13–20.

Coffey, D. (1992) *Schools and Work: Developments in Vocational Education*. London: Cassell.

Covington, M. V. (1992) *Making the Grade: A Self Worth Perspective on Motivation and School Reform*. Cambridge: The Press Syndicate of the University of Cambridge.

Crowther Report 15–18 (1959) *Report of the Minister of Education's Central Advisory Committee*. London: HMSO.

Crozier, M. and Friedberg, E. (1980) *Actors and Systems*. University of Chicago.

Dale, R. (1985) *Education, Training and Employment: Towards a New Vocationalism?* Oxford: Pergamon.

Darkes, D. and Silvester, M. (1994) 'Funding for Enterprise', *Capability*, **1(2)**, 24–32.

Dearing, R. (1993) *The National Curriculum and its Assessment*. London: The Schools Curriculum and Assessment Authority.

Dearing, R. (1995) *Post-16 Qualifications: Interim Review*. London: The Schools Curriculum and Assessment Authority.

Department of Education, Northern Ireland (1992) *Review of Initial Teacher Training in Northern Ireland*.

DES (1963) *Half our Future: A Report of the Central Advisory Council for Education (England)*. London: HMSO.

DES (1984) *Records of Achievement: A Statement of Policy*. London: HMSO.

DES (1988) *Advancing A-Levels*. London: HMSO.

DES (1989) *Further Education: A New Strategy*. London: HMSO.

DES (1991) *Education Statistics for the United Kingdom* . London: HMSO.

DfE (1991) *Education and Training for the 21st Century*. London: HMSO.

Department of Employment (DoE) (1993) *Development of Transferable Skills in Learners*. Research and Development Report No. 18, ED Methods Strategy Unit.

Department of Employment (DoE) (1994) *Higher Education Projects Digest,* Issue 1.

Donald, J. (1992) 'Dewey-eyed optimism: the possibility of democratic education'. *New Left Review*, **192**, 133–44.

Driver, R., *et al.* (1994) 'Constructing Scientific Knowledge in the Classroom', *Educational Researcher*, **23(7)**, 4–12.

Edwards, R. (1989) 'An Experiment in Student Self Assessment', *British Journal of Educational Technology*, **20(1)**, 5–10.

Entwistle, N. (1992) *The Impact of Learning Outcomes in Higher Education*. USDU/ Employment Department.

Evans, B. (1992) *The Politics of the Training Market: From Manpower Services Commission to Training and Enterprise Councils*. London: Routledge.

Evans, J. and Davies, B. (1988) 'The Rise and Fall of Vocational Education', in Pollard, A., Purvis, J. and Wallford, G. (eds) *Education, Training and The New Vocationalism*. Milton Keynes: Open University Press.

Fazey, D. (1993) 'Self Assessment as a Generic Skill for Enterprising Students', *Assessment and Evaluation in Higher Education*, **18(3)**, 235–50.

FEFC (1994) *General Vocational Qualifications in the Further Education Sector in England*. London: FEFC.

Fenwick, A., *et al.* (1992) *Profiling in Higher Education*. London: CNAA.

FEU (1979) *A Basis For Choice*.

FEU (1994) *GNVQs 1993–94 A National Survey Report*. FEU, the Institute of Education London University and The Nuffield Foundation.

FEU/OFSTED (1994) *16–19 Guidance*. London: OFSTED.

Finegold, D., *et al.* (1990) *A British Baccalaureate: Ending the Division between Education and Training*. London: IPPR.

Fleming, D. (1991) 'The Concept of Meta-Competence', *Competence and Assessment*, **16**, 9–12.

Foucault, M. (1977) *Discipline and Punish*. Harmondsworth: Penguin.

Freire, P. (1972) *Pedagogy of the Oppressed*. Harmondsworth: Penguin.

Fullan, M. (1991) *The New Meaning of Educational Change*. London: Cassell.

Fullan, M. (1993) *Change Forces, Probing the Depths of Educational Reform*. Lewes: Falmer.

Giroux, H. (1988) *Schooling and the Struggles for Public Life: Critical Pedagogy in the Modern Age*. University of Minnesota Press.

Gleeson, D. (1980) 'Streaming at work and college; on the social differentiation of craft and technician apprentices in technical education'. *Sociological Review*, **28(4)**, 745–61.

Gleeson, D. (1990) 'Skills Training and Its Alternatives', in Gleeson, D. (ed.) *Training and its Alternatives*. Milton Keynes: Open University Press.

Gleeson, D. and Hodkinson, P. (1995) 'Ideology and Curriculum Policy: GNVQ and Mass Post-Compulsory Education in England and Wales', *British Journal of Education and Work*. (in press)

Green, A. (1991) 'Expanding Public Education', in *Education Limited*. Department of Cultural Studies, University of Birmingham. London: Unwin Hyman.

Green, A. (1993) *Educational Achievement in Britain, France and Japan – A Comparative Analysis*, Institute of Education Working Paper No. 14. University of London.

Green, A. (1995) 'The European Challenge to British Vocational Education and Training', in, Hodkinson, P. and Issitt, M. (eds) *The Challenge of Competence: Professionalism through Vocational Education and Training*. London: Cassell.

Habermas, J. (1978) *Knowledge and Human Interest*. London: Heinemann.

Hallinan, P. and Danaher, P. (1994) 'The Effect of Contracted Grades on Self Efficacy and Motivation in Teacher Education Courses', *Education Research*, **36(1)**, 75–82.

Halsall, R. (1994) 'Moving Forward: Recording Achievement in Higher Education', *Capability*, **1(2)**, 18–23.

Hammersley, M. (1993) 'An Appraisal of Teacher Research', in Hammersley, M. (ed.) *Educational Research: Current Issues*. London: Open University/Paul Chapman.

Harber, C. and Meighan, R. (eds) (1989) *The Democratic School: Educational Management and the Practice of Democracy*. Ticknall: Education Now.

Hargreaves, A. (1986) 'Record Breakers?', in Broadfoot, P. (ed.), *Profiles and Records of Achievement: A Review of Issues and Practices*. London: Cassell.

Hargreaves, A. (1994) *Changing Teachers, Changing Times: Teachers' Work and Culture in the Postmodern Age*. London: Cassell.

Harter, S. (1993) 'Causes and Consequences of Low Self-Esteem in Children and Adolescents', in Baumeister, R. F. (ed.) *Self-Esteem: The Puzzle of Low Self-Regard*. London: Plenum Press.

Hartley, D. (1992) 'The Compacts Initiative: Values for Money?', *British Journal of Educational Studies*, **40(4)**, 321–35.

Harvard, G. and Dunne, R. (1995) 'Competences and Partnership', in Hodkinson, P. and Issitt, M. (eds) *The Challenge of Competence: Professionalism through Vocational Education and Training*. London: Cassell.

Hatch, G. and Shiu, C. (1992) *'Using Games in the Mathematics Classroom'*. International Congress for Mathematics Education Conference, Quebec.

Hayes, G. (1994) 'Core Skills and Grading Within GNVQ', *Achievement*, **Summer**, 19–22.

Heider, F. (1958) The *Psychology of Interpersonal Relations*. New York: Wiley.

Heywood, J. (1994) *Enterprise Learning and its Assessment in Higher Education*. Cambridge: Pendragon Press.

Hjorth, S. (1995) *Coherence Between Compulsory Education, Initial and Continuing Training and Adult Education in Sweden*. Berlin: Panorama, National Report CEDEFOP.

HMI (1989) *Post-16 Education and Training – Core Skills*. London: DES.

Hodkinson, P. (1989) 'Crossing the Academic–Vocational Divide: Personal Effectiveness and Autonomy, as an Integrating Theme in Post-16 Education'. *British Journal of Educational Studies*, **37(4)**, 369–83.

Hodkinson, P. (1991) 'Contexts and Innovation: A Case Study of the Use of CPVE with A-level students', *Educational Studies*, **17(2)**, 191–203.

Hodkinson, P. (1991) 'Liberal Education and the New Vocationalism: A Progressive Partnership?' *Oxford Review of Education*, **17(1)**, 73–88.

Hodkinson, P. (1992) 'Alternative models of competence in vocational education and training', *Journal of Further and Higher Education*, **16(2)**, 30–39.

Hodkinson, P. (1994) 'Empowerment as an entitlement in the post-16 curriculum', *Journal of Curriculum Studies*, **26(5)**, 491–508.

Hodkinson, P. and Hodkinson, H. (1995) 'Markets, Outcomes and VET Quality: some lessons from a Youth Credits Pilot Scheme', *Vocational Aspects of Education*. (in press)

Hodkinson, P. and Issitt, M. (1995) (eds) *The Challenge of Competence: Professionalism Through Vocational Education and Training*. London: Cassell.

Hodkinson, P. and Sparkes, A. C. (1993) 'Prevocationalism and Empowerment: some questions for PE', in Evans, J. (ed.) *Equality and Physical Education*. Lewes: Falmer.

Hodkinson, P. and Sparkes, A. C. (1994) 'The Myth of the Market: The Negotiation of Training in a Youth Credits Pilot Scheme', *British Journal of Education and Work*, **7(3)**, 2–20.

Hodkinson, P. and Sparkes, A. C. (1995a) 'Taking Credits: A Case Study of the Guidance Process into a Training Credits Scheme', *Research Papers in Education*, **10(1)**, 75–99.

Hodkinson, P. and Sparkes, A. C. (1995b) 'Markets and Vouchers: the Inadequacy of Individualist Policies for Vocational Education and Training in England and Wales', *Journal of Educational Policy*, **10(2)** 189–207.

Hollands, R. (1991) 'Working Class Transition: schooling and the training paradigm', in *Education Limited*. Department of Cultural Studies, Birmingham University. London: Unwin Hyman.

Holt, M. and Reid, W. (1988) 'Instrumentalism and education: 14–18 rhetoric and the 11-16 curriculum', in Pollard, A., Purvis, J. and Wallford, G. (eds) *Education, Training and The New Vocationalism*. Milton Keynes: Open University Press.

Howard, R. W. (1987) *Concepts and Schemata: an Introduction*. London: Cassell.

Hustler, D. and Roden M. (1993) *An Evaluation of Flexible Learning in the North West*. Manchester: The Manchester Metropolitan University.

Hustler, D., Milroy, E. and Cockett, M. (1991) *Learning Environments for the Whole Curriculum: It's Not Like Normal Lessons*. London: Unwin Hyman.

Hustler, D., Carter, K., Green, J. and Halsall, R. (1994a) *The Recording Achievement and Higher Education Project*. Cheltenham: UCAS/Employment Department.

Hustler, D., *et al*. (1994b) *Guidance and Learner Autonomy Theme: Interim Evaluation Report*. Manchester: The Manchester Metropolitan University.

Hyland, T. (1991) 'Taking Care of Business: Vocationalism, Competence and the Enterprise Culture', *Educational Studies*, **17(1)**, 77–87.

Hyland, T. (1994) *Competence, Education and NVQs: Dissenting Perspectives*. London: Cassell.

Institute for Public Policy Research (1990) *A British Baccalaureat: Ending the Division between Education and Training*. London: IPPR.

Issitt, M. (1995) 'Competence and the Challenge of Equal Opportunities', in Hodkinson, P. and Issitt, M. (eds) *The Challenge of Competence: Professionalism Through Vocational Education and Training*. London: Cassell.

James, M. (1989) 'Negotiation and dialogue in student assessment and teacher appraisal', in Simons, H. and Elliott, J. (eds) *Rethinking Appraisal and Assessment*. Milton Keynes: Open University Press.

Jamieson, I. (1985) 'Corporate Hegemony or Pedagogic Liberation: the schools-industry movement in England and Wales', in Dale, R. (ed.) *Education, Training and Employment: Towards a New Vocationalism?* Oxford: Pergamon.

Jessup, G. (1991) *Outcomes: NVQs and the Emerging Model of Education and Training*. Lewes: Falmer.

Jones, A. (1989) 'The Real Aims of TVEI', *Education*, **173(15)**, 351–52.

Jones, J. (1995) 'Professional Artistry and Child Protection: Towards a Reflective, Holistic Practice', in Hodkinson, P. and Issitt, M. (eds) *The Challenge of Competence: Professionalism Through Vocational Education and Training*. London: Cassell.

Jones, L. and Moore, R. (1993) 'Education, Competence and the Control of Expertise', *British Journal of the Sociology of Education*, **14(4)**, 385–97.

Keogh, B. and Naylor, S. (1993) 'Learning in Science: Another Way In', *Primary Science Review*, **26(2)**, 22–23.

Keogh, B. and Naylor, S. (1995) *'Cartoons as a Teaching and Learning Approach in Science'*. Proceedings of the European Conference for Research in Science Education, Leeds University.

Kemmis, S. (1983) 'Empowering people: a note on the politics of action research', in Pitman, A., *et al.* (eds) *Educational Enquiry: Approaches to Research*. Deakin University.

Knowles, M. (1981) 'Preface', in Boud, D. (ed.) *Developing Student Autonomy in Learning*. London: Kogan Page.

Kolb, D. (1983) *Experiential Learning: Experience as the Source of Learning and Development*. New York: Prentice Hall.

Kyriacou, C. (1992) 'Active Learning in Secondary School Mathematics', *British Education Research Journal*, **18(3)** 309–18.

Lawton, D. (1994) *The Tory Mind On Education 1979–94*. Lewes: Falmer.

Lee, D., Marsden, D., Rickman, P. and Duncombe, J. (1990) *Scheming for Youth: A study of YTS in the Enterprise Culture*. Milton Keynes: Open University Press.

McCulloch, R. (1993) 'Some Institutional and Practical Implications of Introducing Records of Achievement', in Assiter, A. and Shaw, E. (eds) *Using Records of Achievement in Higher Education*. London: Kogan Page.

Macfarlane, E. (1993) *Education 16–19: In Transition*. London: Routledge.

McLaren, P. (1989) *Life in Schools: An Introduction to Critical Pedagogy in the Foundations of Education*. Harlow: Longman.

Maclure, S. (1991) *Missing Links: The Challenge to Further Education*. London: Policy Studies Institute.

Manchester LEA/NPRA (1992) *Agents Report Form*.

Manchester Metropolitan University (1993a) *Policy for the Professional Preparation of Teachers*. Internal paper.

Manchester Metropolitan University (1993b) *Report on the Recording of Achievement at North Manchester High School for Girls*.

Manchester Metropolitan University (1994) *Report on the Recording of Achievement at City College, Manchester: Community Care curriculum Area*.

Marshall, I. (1991) 'Student driven learning contracts', *Careers Officer*, **2(4)**, 17.

Ministry of Education (1959) *15 to 18: A Report of the Central Advisory* Council for Education. London: HMSO.

Moore, R. (1990) 'Knowledge, Practice and the Construction of Skill,' in Gleeson, D. (ed.) *Training and Its Alternatives*. Milton Keynes: Open University Press.

Morgan, R. (1993) *Crossmaps: An Answer in the Core Skills Debate*. Unpublished paper.

Mortimore, P. and Keane, A. (1986) 'Records of Achievement' in Broadfoot, P. (ed.) *Profiles and Records of Achievement: A Review of Issues and Practice*. London: Cassell.

Munby, S. (1989) *Assessing and Recording Achievement*. Oxford: Blackwell.

Murray, R. (1989) 'Fordism and Post-Fordism', in Hall, S. and Jacques, M. (eds) *New Times: The Changing Face of Politics in the 1990s*. London: Lawrence and Wishart.

National Commission on Education (1993) *Learning to Succeed: A Radical Look at Education Today and A Strategy for the Future*. London: Heinemann.

NCC (National Curriculum Council) (1990) *Core Skills 16–19: A Response to the Secretary of State*. York: NCC.

OCEA (Oxford Consortium for Educational Achievement) (1992) *The OCEA Handbook*.

OFSTED (1994) *GNVQs in Schools, 1993–4*. London: HMSO.

Otter, S. (1992) *Learning Outcomes in Higher Education*. Leicester: UDACE.

Pintrich, P. R. and De Groot, E. V. (1990) 'Motivational and Self Regulated Learning Components of Classroom Academic Performance', *Journal of Educational Psychology*, **82(1)**, 33–40.

Pole, C. (1993) *Assessing and Recording Achievement*. Buckingham: Open University Press.

Pollard, A., Purvis, J. and Wallford, G. (eds) (1988) *Education, Training and the New Vocationalism*. Milton Keynes: Open University Press.

PRAISE (1988) *Records of Achievement: Report of the National Evaluation of Pilot Schemes*. London: DES/Welsh Office.

Raffe, D. (1985) 'Education and Training Initiatives for 14–18s: Content and Context', in Watts, A. G. (ed.) *Education and Training 14–18: Policy and Practice*. Cambridge: CRAC.

RANSC (1989) *Records of Achievement: Report of the Records of Achievement National Steering Committee*. London: DES/Welsh Office.

Research International (1993) *Evaluation of the National Record of Achievement: Use and Experience in Selection*. Employment Department/DfE.

Resnick, L. (1987a) 'Learning in School and Out', *Educational Researcher*, **16(9)**, 13–20.

Resnick, L. (1987b) *Education and Learning to Think*. Washington, DC: National Academy Press.

(ROAHE) Recording of Achievement and Higher Education Project (1994) *A Collection of Case Studies*. Wigan: ROAHE Project.

Robertson, D. (1992) 'Courses, Qualifications and the Empowerment of Learners' in Finegold, D., *et al*. (eds) *Higher Education: Expansion and Reform*. London: Institute for Public Policy Research.

Robertson, D. (1994) *Choosing to Change*. London: HEQC.

Rogers, C. (1969) *Freedom to Learn*. Oxford: Merrill.

Saunders, M. and Halpin, D. (1990) 'TVEI and The National Curriculum: A Cautionary Note', in *TVEI and the National Curriculum*, a conference report. University of Exeter.

Schunk, D. and Gaa, J. (1981) 'Goal Setting Influence on Learning and Self Evaluation', *Journal of Classroom Interaction*, **16(2)**, 38–44.

Senker, P. (1995) *The Development and Implication of National Vocational Qualifications: An Engineering Case Study*. (mimeo)

Shaw, K. and Bloomer, M. (1993) 'Guidance and Transition at 16+', *Journal of Further and Higher Education*, **17** (1), 80–91.

Smithers, A. (1993) *All Our Futures: Britain's Education Revolution*. Channel 4 Television.

Spours, K. (1992) *Recent Developments in Qualifications at 14+: A Critical Review*. Working paper No. 12: Institute of Education, University of London.

Spours, K. and Young, M. (1990) 'Beyond Vocationalism: A New Perspective on the Relationship Between Work and Education', in Gleeson, D. (ed.) *Training and Its Alternatives*. Milton Keynes: Open University Press.

Spours, K. and Young, M. (1994) *Enhancing the Post-16 Curriculum: Value Added*

Perspectives. The Post 16 Centre, The Institute of Education, London University.

Stansbury, D. (1980) 'The Record of Personal Experience', in Burgess, T. and Adams, E. (eds) *Outcomes of Education.* London: Macmillan.

Steedman, H. and Hawkins, J. (1994) 'Shifting Foundations: the Impact of NVQs on Youth Training for the Building Trades', *National Institute Economic Review,* **August,** 93–102.

Stenhouse, L. (1975) *An Introduction to Curriculum Research and Development.* London: Heinemann.

Stronach, I. (1989) 'A Critique of the New Assessment', in Simons, H. and Elliott, J. (eds) *Rethinking Appraisal and Assessment.* Milton Keynes: Open University Press.

Taylor, M. J. (1992) 'Post-16 Option: Young People's Awareness, Attitudes, Intentions and Influences on their Choice', *Research Papers in Education,* **7(3),** 301–35.

TES (1995) 'A Rare Outbreak of Harmony,' **21 July.**

THES (1994) 'Trojan Horse Mired in A-level Mud', **4 November.**

Tomlinson, P. and Kilner, S. (1991) *The Flexible Learning Framework and Current Educational Theory.* London: The Employment Department.

Training Agency (1988) *The Compact Development Handbook.* London: HMSO.

University of Portsmouth (1993) *National Project Directory: Enterprise in Higher Education.*

Ward, D. and Mullender, A. (1991) 'Empowerment and Oppression: An Indissoluble Pairing for Contemporary Social work', *Critical Social Policy,* **Issue 32,** 21–30.

Weick, K. E. (1979) *The Social Psychology of Organising.* New York: Random House.

Weiner, B. and Kukla, A. (1970) 'An Attributional Analysis of Achievement Motivation', *Journal of Personal and Social Psychology,* **15,** 1–20.

Weston, P. (1988) *Lower Attaining Pupils Programme National Evaluation: The Search for Success.* Slough: NFER.

White Paper (1994) *Competitiveness: Helping Business to Win.* London: HMSO.

White Paper (1995) *Forging Ahead.* London: HMSO.

Williams, K. (1994) 'Vocationalism and Liberal Education: exploring the tensions', *Journal of Philosophy of Education,* **28(1),** 89–100.

Winter, R. (1992) 'Quality Management or The Educative Workplace: Alternative Versions of Competence-Based Education', *Journal of Further and Higher Education,* **16(3),** 100–115.

Wolf, A. (1995) *Competence-Based Assessment.* Buckingham: Open University Press.

Young, M. (1971) *Knowledge and Control.* London: Collier–Macmillan.

Young, M. (1993a) 'A Curriculum for the 21st Century? Towards a New Basis For Overcoming Academic/Vocational Divisions', *British Journal of Educational Studies,* **41(3),** 203–22.

Young, M. (1993b) 'Bridging the Academic/Vocational Divide: Two Nordic Case Studies', *European Journal of Education,* **28(2),** 209–14.

Young, M. (1994) 'What kind of 14-19 System?', *Post-16 Education Newsletter,* **No. 8.** Institute of Education, University of London.

Zimmerman, B. J. (1989) 'Social Cognitive View of Self Regulated Learning', *Journal of Educational Psychology,* **81(3),** 329–39.

Index

A-levels 2, 9, 12, 15, 58, 70, 75, 81, 88, 125, 126, 142
academic–vocational divide 8, 50, 80–84
action planning 93, 94
Adams, E. 90, 105
alternative curricula 7, 33–49
Alternative Curriculum Strategies Project 38
assessment 20, 21, 26–29, 31, 42, 88, 89, 91, 95, 96, 99, 100, 103, 106, 107, 129
ASSET 86, 88
Avis, J. 68, 81, 83, 111, 115

Baker, K. 74
Ball, C. 114, 125
Barnes, D. 108, 110
Barnett, R. 18, 80, 86
Barrow, R. 78
Berkeley, J. 91, 105
Bridges, D. 79, 80, 87
Broadfoot, P. 89, 91, 101
BTEC 27, 31, 71, 74, 76
Burgess, T. 90, 105

Callaghan, J. 7, 50–72, 138, 139
CBI 11, 14, 73, 75
citizenship 15, 110, 126
Coates, P. 73, 78, 79
Cockett, M. 7, 9, 10, 33–49, 50–72, 137–142
Coffey, D. 33, 34, 50
compacts 3, 39, 40
competences 17–32, 84–88, 123
competitiveness 3, 16, 123
continuity 11, 51, 68, 107, 117–119, 137, 139–141
core skills 8, 31, 73–88, 112, 114
    A-levels 4, 75, 88
    academic–vocational divide 80–84
    GNVQs 75–77, 88
    mandatory 76
    optional 76, 88
    transferability 77–79
Covington, M. 54, 55, 71
CPVE 74, 113
CROSSMAPS 75
Crowther Report 6, 12, 35
curriculum breadth 3, 8, 31, 48, 73, 82, 84, 85

Dearing, R. 2, 3, 46, 50, 70, 71, 81, 82, 117, 141
DES 90, 109
DfE 2, 109, 114
DfEE 141
differentiation 38

Employment Department 2, 32, 78, 109, 114, 121, 126, 128–130, 139
empowerment 15, 94, 102, 104, 108, 110, 111, 115, 116, 123, 124, 133
Entwistle, N. 108–110, 112, 118
Enterprise in Higher Education 93, 109, 113, 114, 126, 128

FEFC 13, 14, 54, 81
Fleming, D. 79, 80
Foucault, M. 103
functional analysis 19, 20, 84

GCSE 2, 14, 71, 89, 138
  grading system 39, 45, 48,
    51–53, 56–63, 66–68
General Education Diploma
  82, 140
Gleeson, D. 6, 7, 11–16, 24, 34,
  66, 70, 140, 142
GNVQs 2, 4, 12, 35, 36, 40, 41,
  45, 46, 49–51, 58, 68, 71,
  75–77, 81, 82, 84, 87, 88, 125,
  126, 130
Green, A. 31, 50, 67

Halsall, R. 1–10, 28, 73–88,
  89–107, 113, 120–136, 138–141
Hargreaves, A. 27, 48, 102–105,
  139
Harter, S. 54
higher education 9, 12, 85–87,
  98, 99, 109, 117, 120–136,
  138–140
  barriers to change 131–135
  Credit Frameworks and
    Learning Outcomes
    Theme 130
  forces for change 121–126
  Guidance and Learner
    Autonomy Theme 109,
    129, 131–135
  Higher Education Projects
    Fund 126, 128–130
  records of achievement 120,
    127, 128
  Work Based Learning Theme
    129, 130
Hodkinson, P. 7, 9, 17–32, 33,
  49, 67, 70, 83, 84, 108–119,
  138, 140, 141
Hustler, D. 9, 38, 96, 98,
  108–136, 138, 140, 141

Hyland, T. 18, 66, 80–82

Initial Teacher Training 42, 85,
  86, 88
Institute for Public Policy
  Research 82
Issitt, M. 18, 28, 29

Jamieson, I. 114, 115
Jones, L. 84

Knowles, M. 92, 123
Kolb, D. 112, 122
Kyriacou, C. 108, 109

labour market 17, 22
Lawton, D. 47, 49, 50
learner autonomy 77, 83, 85,
  92, 93, 100, 101, 108, 109, 110,
  114–116, 119, 134, 135, 140,
  141
learning contracts 69, 70
liberal education 34, 35, 36, 42,
  87
Local Education Authorities 1,
  106, 109
local management of schools
  3, 14
lower attainers 7, 33–49
Lower Attaining Pupils Project
  35, 37–39, 41, 43, 44, 46, 49,
  110, 113

Macfarlane, E. 5, 73, 75
Maclure, S. 12, 74
Manchester LEA 106
Manchester Metropolitan
  University 85, 95, 96, 101, 106
markets 6, 13–15, 25, 115, 116,
  139

metacompetences 79, 80
modern apprenticeships 3, 24
modularity 58, 71, 82, 116, 123, 124, 126, 133
Moore, R. 36, 84
motivation 8, 39, 44, 49, 53–62, 91, 92, 99
Munby, S. 92
Murray, R. 4

National Commission on Education 50, 82, 140
National Curriculum 3, 8, 46–48, 81, 117
National Training and Education Targets 2, 7, 13, 22, 25, 89, 123
National Curriculum Council 75
NCVQ 2, 7, 17, 18, 20, 23, 26, 30–32, 40, 75, 77, 80, 81, 85, 87, 88, 90, 122, 123
negotiation 103, 104, 108, 112
New Educational Settlement 15, 140, 142
New Training Initiative 123
Newsom Report 35–37, 41, 43, 45, 49
NVQs 1, 2, 7, 17–32, 71, 115, 123, 129, 130, 138
OFSTED 54, 81
Oxford Consortium for Educational Achievement 106

parental choice 49
parity of esteem 6, 11, 15, 41, 70, 140
performance criteria 28, 31, 76, 80

Pole, C. 90, 95, 100, 104
post-Fordism 4, 8, 33, 74, 89
PRAISE 90, 94–96, 99–101
progression 1, 8, 10, 41, 62–66, 68, 69, 107, 126, 137, 139–142

Raffe, D. 44, 45
Raising of the School Leaving Age 35, 36
Recording Achievement and Higher Education Project 91, 96, 98, 107, 109, 126–128
Records of Achievement 4, 8, 39, 47, 89–107, 138, 141
  assessment 91, 95, 96
  autonomy 92–94, 100, 101
  control 102–104
  end-users 91, 96–99
  higher education 98, 99, 120, 126–128
  motivation 92, 99
  ownership 102
  privacy 101, 102
  quality assurance 105, 106
reductivism 84–88
relevance 33, 34, 36, 37, 49, 91, 114, 124
Research International 96
Resnick, L. 25, 31, 78
reviewing 93, 100, 101
Robertson, D. 124, 133

School Curriculum and Assessment Authority 2, 8, 41, 81
School Examinations and Assessment Council 75
self-esteem 54, 56, 61, 92
Smithers, A. 26, 80, 84
Sparkes, A. 22, 70, 113, 116

Spours, K. 34, 49, 50, 68
status (of courses) 34, 44, 45,
    47, 48, 83, 84, 113, 115, 130,
    140
Stronach, I. 103
student-centredness 9, 16, 102,
    108–119, 140
    democracy 110, 111
    effective learning 111–114
    empowerment 110, 111
    records of achievement 92
    vocationalism 114–119

training credits 13, 22–24, 32
training levies 14
training providers 22, 24–27,
    30, 116
training quality 18, 24, 25, 30

transferability 8, 77–79, 88
transition 50–72, 139
TVEI 3, 39, 47, 48, 93, 110, 113,
    114, 117

values 28, 75, 85–87
vocationalism 7, 14, 33–49,
    114–116

Weston, P. 37–39, 44
White Papers 2, 11, 12, 50, 72,
    81
Winter, R. 87

Young, M. 34, 48–50, 62, 67, 68,
    70
Youth Training 3, 26, 32, 34,
    104

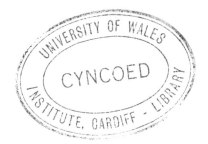